Quick and Easy, Prs

Healthy
Salads

Publisher's Note: Raw or semi-cooked eggs should not be consumed by babies, toddlers, pregnant or breastfeeding women, the elderly or those suffering from a chronic illness.

Publisher & Creative Director: Nick Wells
Senior Project Editor: Catherine Taylor
Editorial: Esme Chapman
Art Director: Mike Spender
Layout Design: Jane Ashley
Digital Design & Production: Chris Herbert

Special thanks to Laura Bulbeck, Emma Chafer and Frances Bodiam.

This is a **FLAME TREE** Book

FLAME TREE PUBLISHING
Crabtree Hall, Crabtree Lane
Fulham, London SW6 6TY
United Kingdom
www.flametreepublishing.com

First published 2014

ISBN: 978-1-78361-243-7

Printed in Singapore

All images are courtesy of Flame Tree Publishing Limited except the following which are courtesy of **Shutterstock.com** and © the following contributors: 22 Maryna Pleshkun; 23 Mariusz Szczygiel; 24 D. Pimborough; 33 Liv friis-larsen; 37 sarsmis; 41, 59, 77 A_Lein; 45 Ildi Papp; 49, 181, 229 marco mayer; 53 Yevgeniya Shal; 55 vanillaechoes; 61, 65, 119 margouillat photo; 67, 187 ElenaGaak; 69 Nitr; 73 Frank L Junior; 83 Tungphoto; 85 Catherine Murray; 89 Stanislav Komogorov; 91 photka; 95 Zigzag Mountain Art; 99 Fanfo; 103 Magdanatka; 109 Lesya Dolyuk; 111 Lapina Maria; 115 AlenaKogotkova; 117, 195 Patty Orly; 121 Mshev; 125 Fernando Sanchez Cortes; 127 alexsalcedo; 133, 141 Shebeko; 135 Iryna Melnyk; 137 eugena-klykova; 145 TatyanaPanova; 149 B. and E. Dudzinscy; 151, 157 nito; 155 fotoedu; 159 Ewa Sek; 169 Timolina; 175 Piccia Neri; 193 Netfalls - Remy Musser; 199 MSPhotographic; 201 Olaf Speier; 205 Stephanie Frey.

Quick and Easy, Proven Recipes

Healthy Salads

FLAME TREE
PUBLISHING

Contents

*

Introduction

Healthy salads? Surely, all salads are healthy, but no, it all depends on the ingredients used. Some, in fact, can be considerably unhealthy and can pile on the calories without you realising, especially if a salad dressing is added to the salad, as this can have more calories than the salad itself due to its fat content. So, what can you do to make salads healthy and interesting and not rely on just tomatoes, lettuce and cucumber?

There are many different types of salad that are simple to prepare and can be enjoyed in today's lifestyle. Salads have moved on considerably since the 1980s, when it was just three ingredients accompanied by a slice of cold meat, a little grated cheese or a sliced hard-boiled egg. Salads have blossomed and there is now a tremendous array of different ingredients from around the world that can be incorporated into a salad, such as quinoa from South America, couscous from North Africa, tofu from China, and plump ripe black Kalamata olives and delicious olive oil from Greece, to name just a few. Why not try Falafel Salad with Houmous & Olives (*see* page 174) or Thai Beef & Chilli Salad (*see* page 82) or Tofu & Sesame Salad (*see* page 48) or Mussel & Tuna Salad on page 144?

There are a host of ingredients that can be used together, which perhaps have not been thought of as salad before, such as Bulgur Wheat, Liver & Clementine (*see* page 120), Apple & Cranberry Chicken Salad (*see* page 94), or Hot Grilled Chicory & Pears (*see* page 248). This book is also ideal for anyone following a healthy eating plan, as there is a whole chapter dedicated to guilt-free salads. Choose from the classic Waldorf Salad or the Grilled Salmon Caesar with Seeded Crackers (*see* page 72) to favourites including a Greek salad or fruity salads, such as Strawberry, Baby Spinach & Feta Salad (*see* page 68).

As well as having 100 delicious recipes, there are clear, concise and easy-to-follow instructions with each recipe. Plus, in the front of the book, there is a helpful section on hygiene in the kitchen as well as nutritional and healthy eating advice, so enjoy creating and eating healthy salads.

Essentials

Easy to prepare and delicious to eat, salads offer a great cooking and dining experience. But before you get started on discovering which salad to try next, check out the handy information this chapter has to offer. Start by getting to grips with hygiene in the kitchen before brushing up on your nutritional knowledge and healthy eating guidelines. In no time, you will know how to choose from the recipes that follow to optimise your health and wellbeing.

Hygiene in the Kitchen

I t is well worth remembering that many foods can carry some form of bacteria. In most cases, the worst it will lead to is a bout of food poisoning or gastroenteritis, although for certain people this can be more serious. The risk can be reduced or eliminated by good food hygiene and proper cooking.

Do not buy food that is past its sell-by date and do not consume any food that is past its use-by date. When buying food, use your eyes and nose. If the food looks tired, limp or a bad colour or it has a rank, acrid or simply bad smell, do not buy or eat it under any circumstances. Do take special care when preparing raw meat and fish.

A separate chopping board should be used for each food; wash the knife, board and the hands thoroughly before handling or preparing any other food.

Regularly clean, defrost and clear out the refrigerator or freezer – it is worth checking the packaging to see exactly how long each product is safe to freeze.

Avoid handling food if suffering from an upset stomach, as bacteria can be passed on through food preparation.

Dishcloths and tea towels must be washed and changed regularly. Ideally, use disposable cloths, which should be replaced on a daily basis. More durable cloths should be left to soak in bleach, then washed in the washing machine on a boil wash.

Keep hands, cooking utensils and food preparation surfaces clean and do not allow pets to climb onto any work surfaces.

Buying

Avoid bulk buying where possible, especially fresh produce such as meat, poultry, fish, fruit and vegetables, unless buying for the freezer. Fresh foods lose their nutritional value rapidly, so buying a little at a time minimises loss of nutrients. It also eliminates a packed refrigerator, which reduces the effectiveness of the refrigeration process.

When buying prepackaged goods such as cans or pots of cream and yogurts, check that the packaging is intact and not damaged or pierced at all. Cans should not be dented, pierced or rusty. Check the sell-by dates even for cans and packets of dry ingredients such as flour and rice. Store fresh foods in the refrigerator as soon as possible – not in the car or the office.

When buying frozen foods, ensure that they are not heavily iced on the outside and the contents feel completely frozen. Ensure that the frozen foods have been stored in the cabinet at the correct storage level and the temperature is below -18˚C/-0.4˚F. Pack in cool bags to transport home and place in the freezer as soon as possible after purchase.

Preparation

Make sure that all work surfaces and utensils are clean and dry. Hygiene should be given priority at all times. Separate chopping boards should be used for raw and cooked meats, fish and vegetables. Currently, a variety of good-quality plastic boards come in various designs and colours. This makes differentiating easier and the plastic has the added hygienic

advantage of being washable at high temperatures in the dishwasher. (NB: If using the board for fish, first wash in cold water, then in hot, to prevent odour!) Also, remember that knives and utensils should always be thoroughly cleaned after use.

When cooking, be particularly careful to keep cooked and raw food separate to avoid any contamination. It is worth washing all fruits and vegetables, regardless of whether they are going to be eaten raw or lightly cooked. This rule should apply even to prewashed herbs and salads.

Do not reheat food more than once. If using a microwave, always check that the food is piping hot all the way through. In theory, the food should reach a minimum temperature of 70°C/158°F and needs to be cooked at that temperature for at least three minutes to ensure that any bacteria in the food are killed.

All poultry must be thoroughly thawed before using, including chicken and poussin. Remove the food to be thawed from the freezer and place in a shallow dish to contain the juices.

Leave the food in the refrigerator until it is completely thawed. A 1.4 kg/3 lb whole chicken will take about 26–30 hours to thaw. To speed up the process, immerse the chicken in cold water. However, make sure that the water is changed regularly. When the joints can move freely and no ice crystals remain in the cavity, the bird is completely thawed.

Once thawed, remove the wrapper and pat the chicken dry. Place the chicken in a shallow dish, cover lightly and, if storing, store as close to the base of the refrigerator as possible. The chicken should be cooked as soon as possible.

Some foods can be cooked from frozen, including many prepacked foods such as soups, sauces, casseroles and breads. Where applicable, follow the manufacturers' instructions.

Vegetables and fruits can also be cooked from frozen, but meats and fish should be thawed first. The only time food can be refrozen is when the food has been thoroughly thawed, then cooked. Once the food has cooled, then it can be frozen again. On such occasions, the food can only be stored for one month.

All poultry and game (except for duck) must be cooked thoroughly. When cooked, the juices will run clear from the thickest part of the bird – the best area to try is usually the thigh. Other meats, such as minced meat and pork, should be cooked right the way through. Fish should turn opaque, be firm in texture and break easily into large flakes.

When cooking leftovers, make sure they are reheated until piping hot and that any sauce or soup reaches boiling point first before eating.

Storing, Refrigerating and Freezing

Meat, poultry, fish, seafood and dairy products should all be refrigerated. The temperature of the refrigerator should be between 1–5°C/34–41°F, while the freezer temperature should not rise above -18°C/-0.4°F.

To ensure the optimum refrigerator and freezer temperature, avoid leaving the door open for a long time. Try not to overstock the refrigerator, as this reduces the airflow inside and affects the

Hygiene in the Kitchen

efficiency in cooling the food within. When refrigerating cooked food, allow it to cool down quickly and completely before refrigerating. Hot food will raise the temperature of the refrigerator and possibly affect or spoil other food stored in it.

Food within the refrigerator and freezer should always be covered. Raw and cooked food should be stored in separate parts of the refrigerator. Cooked food should be kept on the top shelves of the refrigerator, while raw meat, poultry and fish should be placed on the bottom shelves to avoid drips and cross-contamination.

It is recommended that eggs should be refrigerated in order to maintain their freshness and shelf life.

Take care that frozen foods are not stored in the freezer for too long. Blanched vegetables can be stored for one month; beef, lamb, poultry and pork for six months; and unblanched vegetables and fruits in syrup for a year. Oily fish and sausages can be stored for three months. Dairy products can last four to six months, while cakes and pastries can be kept in the freezer for three to six months.

High-risk Foods

Certain foods may carry risks to people who are considered vulnerable, such as the elderly, the ill, pregnant or breastfeeding women, babies, young infants and those suffering from a recurring illness. It is advisable to avoid those foods listed below, which belong to a higher-risk category.

There is a slight chance that some eggs carry the bacteria salmonella. Cook eggs until both the yolk and the white are firm to eliminate this risk.

Pay particular attention to dishes and products incorporating lightly cooked or raw eggs, which should be eliminated from the diet. Sauces including Hollandaise, mayonnaise, mousses, soufflés and meringues all use raw or lightly cooked eggs, as do custard-based dishes, ice creams and sorbets. These are all considered high-risk foods to the vulnerable groups mentioned above.

Certain meats and poultry also carry the potential risk of salmonella and so should be cooked thoroughly until the juices run clear and there is no pinkness left. Unpasteurised products such as milk, cheese (especially soft cheese), pâté and meat (both raw and cooked) all have the potential risk of listeria and should be avoided.

When buying seafood, buy from a reputable source which has a high turnover to ensure freshness. Fish should have bright, clear eyes, shiny skin and bright pink or red gills. The fish should feel stiff to the touch, with a slight smell of sea air and iodine. The flesh of fish steaks and fillets should be translucent, with no signs of discolouration.

Molluscs such as scallops, clams and mussels are sold fresh and are still alive. Avoid any that are open or do not close when tapped lightly. In the same way, univalves such as whelks or winkles should withdraw back into their shells when lightly prodded. When choosing cephalopods such as squid and octopus, they should have firm flesh and a pleasant sea smell.

As with all fish, whether it is shellfish or wet fish, care is required when freezing it. It is imperative to check whether the fish has been frozen before. If it has been frozen, then it should not be frozen again under any circumstances.

Hygiene in the Kitchen

Nutrition

ℰ

Home-cooked meals are a great way to provide us with a healthy and well-balanced diet, the body's primary energy source. In children, a healthy diet is the basis of future health and provides lots of energy. In adults, it encourages self-healing and regeneration within the body. A well-balanced, varied diet will provide the body with all the essential nutrients it needs. The ideal variety of foods is shown in the pyramid below.

Fats
milk, yogurt
and cheese

Proteins
meat, fish, poultry, eggs,
nuts and pulses

*Fruits and
Vegetables*

Starchy Carbohydrates
cereals, potatoes, bread, rice and pasta

Fats

Fats fall into two categories: saturated and unsaturated fats. It is very important that a healthy balance is achieved within the diet. Fats are an essential part of the diet and a source of energy and provide essential fatty acids and fat–soluble vitamins. The right balance of fats should boost the body's immunity to infection and keep muscles, nerves and arteries in good condition. Saturated fats are of animal origin and are hard when stored at room temperature. They can be found in dairy produce, meat, eggs, margarines and hard, white cooking fat (lard) as well as in manufactured products such as pies, biscuits and cakes. A high intake of saturated fat over many years has been proven to increase heart disease and high blood cholesterol levels and often leads to weight gain. The aim of a healthy diet is to keep the fat content low in the foods that we eat. Lowering the amount of saturated fat that we consume is very important, but this does not mean that it is good to consume lots of other types of fat.

There are two kinds of unsaturated fats: polyunsaturated fats and monounsaturated fats. Polyunsaturated fats include the following oils: safflower oil, soybean oil, corn oil and sesame oil. Within the polyunsaturated group are Omega oils. The Omega-3 oils are of significant interest because they have been found to be particularly beneficial to coronary health and can encourage brain growth and development. Omega-3 oils are derived from oily fish such as salmon, mackerel, herring, pilchards and sardines. It is recommended that we should eat these types of fish at least once a week. However, for those who do not eat fish or who are vegetarians, liver oil supplements are available in most supermarkets and health shops. It is suggested that these supplements should be taken on a daily basis. The most popular oils that are high in monounsaturates are olive oil, sunflower oil and peanut oil. The Mediterranean diet, which is based on foods high in monounsaturated fats, is recommended for heart health. Also, monounsaturated fats are known to help reduce the levels of LDL (the bad) cholesterol.

Proteins

Composed of amino acids (proteins' building bricks), proteins perform a wide variety of functions for the body, including supplying energy and building and repairing tissue. Good sources of proteins are eggs, milk, yogurt, cheese, meat, fish, poultry, nuts and pulses. (See the second level of the pyramid.) Some of these foods, however, contain saturated fats. For a nutritional balance, eat generous amounts of soya beans, lentils, peas and nuts.

Fruits and Vegetables

Not only are fruits and vegetables the most visually appealing foods, but they are extremely good for us, providing vital vitamins and minerals essential for growth, repair and protection in the human body. Fruits and vegetables are low

Nutrition

in calories and are responsible for regulating the body's metabolic processes and controlling the composition of its fluids and cells.

Minerals

- ❧ Calcium – Important for healthy bones and teeth, nerve transmission, muscle contraction, blood clotting and hormone function. Calcium promotes a healthy heart, improves skin, relieves aching muscles and bones, maintains the correct acid-alkaline balance and reduces menstrual cramps. Good sources are dairy products, small bones of small fish, nuts, pulses, fortified white flours, breads and green, leafy vegetables.

- ❧ Chromium – Part of the glucose tolerance factor, chromium balances blood sugar levels, helps to normalise hunger and reduce cravings, improves lifespan, helps protect DNA and is essential for heart function. Good sources are brewer's yeast, wholemeal bread, rye bread, oysters, potatoes, green peppers, butter and parsnips.

- ❧ Iodine – Important for healthy thyroid function and for normal development. Good sources of iodine are seafood, seaweed, milk and dairy products.

- ❧ Iron – As a component of haemoglobin, iron carries oxygen around the body. It is vital for normal growth and development. Good sources are liver, corned beef, red meat, fortified breakfast cereals, pulses, green, leafy vegetables, egg yolk and cocoa and cocoa products.

- ❧ Magnesium – Important for efficient functioning of metabolic enzymes and development of the skeleton. Magnesium promotes healthy muscles by helping them to relax and is therefore good for PMS. It is also important for heart muscles and the nervous system. Good sources are nuts, green vegetables, meat, cereals, milk and yogurt.

Phosphorus – Forms and maintains bones and teeth, builds muscle tissue, helps maintain the body's pH and aids metabolism and energy production. Phosphorus is present in almost all foods.

Potassium – Enables nutrients to move into cells, while waste products move out; promotes healthy nerves and muscles; maintains fluid balance in the body; helps secretion of insulin for blood sugar control to produce constant energy; relaxes muscles; maintains heart functioning and stimulates gut movement to encourage proper elimination. Good sources are fruit, vegetables, milk and bread.

Selenium – Antioxidant properties help to protect against free radicals and carcinogens. Selenium reduces inflammation, stimulates the immune system to fight infections, promotes a healthy heart and helps vitamin E's action. It is also required for the male reproductive system and is needed for metabolism. Good sources are tuna, liver, kidney, meat, eggs, cereals, nuts and dairy products.

Sodium – Helps to control body fluid and balance, preventing dehydration. Sodium is involved in muscle and nerve function and helps move nutrients into cells. All foods are good sources, but pickled and salted foods are richest in sodium.

Zinc – Important for metabolism and the healing of wounds. It also aids ability to cope with stress, promotes a healthy nervous system and brain, especially in the growing foetus, aids bone and tooth formation and is essential for constant energy. Good sources are liver, meat, pulses, wholegrain cereals, nuts and oysters.

Nutrition

Vitamins

∞ **Vitamin A** – Important for cell growth and development and for the formation of visual pigments in the eye. Found in liver, meat, whole milk, red and yellow fruits and carrots.

∞ **Vitamin B1** – Important in releasing energy from carbohydrate-containing foods. Good sources are yeast and yeast products, bread, fortified breakfast cereals and potatoes.

∞ **Vitamin B2** – Important for metabolism of proteins, fats and carbohydrates. Found in meat, yeast extract, fortified cereals and milk.

∞ **Vitamin B3** – Helps the metabolism of food into energy. Sources are milk and milk products, fortified breakfast cereals, pulses, meat, poultry and eggs.

∞ **Vitamin B5** – Important for the metabolism of food and energy production. All foods are good sources, but especially fortified breakfast cereals, wholegrain bread and dairy products.

∞ **Vitamin B6** – Important for metabolism of protein and fat. Vitamin B6 may also be involved with the regulation of sex hormones. Good sources are liver, fish, pork, soya beans and peanuts.

∞ **Vitamin B12** – Important for the production of red blood cells and DNA. It is vital for growth and the nervous system. Good sources are meat, fish, eggs, poultry and milk.

∞ **Biotin** – Important for metabolism of fatty acids. Good sources of biotin are liver, kidney, eggs and nuts. Micro-organisms also manufacture this vitamin in the gut.

- Vitamin C – Important for healing wounds and the formation of collagen, which keeps skin and bones strong. It is an important antioxidant. Sources are fruits and vegetables.

- Vitamin D – Important for absorption of calcium to build bone strength. Sources are oily fish, eggs, whole milk and milk products, margarine and sunlight – vitamin D is made in the skin.

- Vitamin E – Important as an antioxidant vitamin, helping to protect cell membranes from damage. Good sources are vegetable oils, margarines, seeds, nuts and green vegetables.

- Folic Acid – Critical during pregnancy for the development of foetus brain and nerves. It is essential for brain and nerve function and is needed for protein and red blood cell formation. Sources are wholegrain cereals, fortified cereals, green, leafy vegetables, oranges and liver.

- Vitamin K – Important for controlling blood clotting. Sources are cauliflower, Brussels sprouts, lettuce, cabbage, beans, broccoli, peas, asparagus, potatoes, corn oil, tomatoes and milk.

Carbohydrates

Carbohydrates come in two basic forms: starchy and sugar carbohydrates. Starchy carbohydrates, also known as complex carbohydrates, include cereals, potatoes, breads, rice and pasta. (See the fourth level of the pyramid). Eating wholegrain varieties also provides fibre, beneficial in preventing bowel cancer, and controlling cholesterol levels. Sugar carbohydrates, known as fast-release carbohydrates (because of the quick fix of energy they give), include sugar and sugar-sweetened products such as jams and syrups. Milk provides lactose, which is milk sugar, and fruits provide fructose, which is fruit sugar.

Guidelines for Different Age Groups

Good food plays such an important role in everyone's life. From infancy through to adulthood, a healthy diet provides the body's foundation and building blocks and teaches children healthy eating habits. Studies have shown that these eating habits stay with us into later life, helping us to maintain a healthier lifestyle as adults. This reduces the risk of illness, disease and certain medical problems.

Striking a healthy balance is important and at certain stages in life, this balance may need to be adjusted to help our bodies cope. As babies and children, during pregnancy and in later life, our diet assists us in achieving optimal health. So, how do we go about achieving this?

We know that food such as oily fish, for example, is advantageous to all, as it is rich in Omega-3 fatty acids which have been linked with more efficient brain functioning and better memory. They can also help lower the risk of cancer and heart disease. But are there any other steps we can take to maximise health benefits through our diet?

Babies and Young Children

Babies should not be given solids until they are at least six months old, then new tastes and textures can be introduced to their diets. Probably the easiest and cheapest way is to adapt the food that the rest of the family eat. Babies under the age of one should be given breast milk or formula milk. From the age of one to two, whole milk should be given, and from two to five, semi-skimmed milk can be given. From then on, skimmed milk can be introduced if desired.

The first foods for babies under six months should be of a purée-like consistency, which is smooth and fairly liquid, therefore making it easy to swallow. This can be done using an electric blender or hand blender or just by pushing foods through a sieve to remove any lumps. Remember, however, babies still need lots of milk.

Babies over six months old should still be having puréed food, but the consistency of their diet can be made progressively lumpier. Around the 10-month mark, most babies are able to manage food cut up into small pieces.

So, what food groups do babies and small children need? Like adults, a high proportion of their diet should contain grains such as cereal, pasta, bread and rice. However, be careful, as babies and small children cannot cope with too much high-fibre food in their diet.

Fresh fruits and vegetables should be introduced, as well as a balance of dairy and meat proteins and only a small proportion of fats and sweets. Research points out that delaying the introduction of foods which could cause allergies during the first year (such as cow's milk, wheat, eggs, cheese, yogurt and nuts) can significantly reduce the risk of certain food allergies later on in life. (NB: Peanuts should never be given to children under five years old.)

Seek a doctor's or health visitor's advice regarding babies and toddlers. Limit sugar in young children's diets, as sugar provides only empty calories. Use less-processed sugars (muscovado is very sweet, so the amount used can be reduced) or incorporate less-refined alternatives such as dried fruits, dates, rice syrup or honey. (NB: Honey should not be given to infants under one year of age.)

As in a low-fat diet, it is best to eliminate fried foods and avoid adding salt – especially for babies under a year old and young infants. Instead, introduce herbs and gentle spices to make food appetising. The more varied the tastes that children experience in their formative years, the wider the range of foods they will accept later in life.

Guidelines

Pregnancy

During pregnancy, women are advised to take extra vitamin and mineral supplements. Pregnant women benefit from a healthy balanced diet, rich in fresh fruit and vegetables, and full of essential vitamins and minerals. Oily fish, such as salmon, not only give the body essential fats, but also provide high levels of bio-available calcium.

Certain food groups, however, hold risks during pregnancy. This section gives advice on everyday foods and those that should be avoided.

∞ Cheese – Pregnant women should avoid all soft mould-ripened cheese such as Brie. Also if pregnant, do not eat cheese such as Parmesan or blue-veined cheese like Stilton, as they carry the potential risk of listeria. It is fine for pregnant women to carry on eating hard cheese like Cheddar, as well as cottage cheese.

∞ Eggs – There is a slight chance that some eggs will carry salmonella. Cooking the eggs until both the yolk and white are firm will eliminate this risk. However, particular attention should be paid to dishes and products that incorporate lightly cooked or raw eggs, home-made mayonnaise or similar sauces, mousses, soufflés, meringues, ice creams and sorbets. Commercially produced products, such as mayonnaise, which are made with pasteurised eggs, may be eaten safely. If in doubt, it's best to avoid it.

∞ Ready-made meals and ready-to-eat items – Previously cooked then chilled meals are now widely available, but those from the chilled counter can contain bacteria. Avoid prepacked salads in dressings and other foods which are sold loose from chill cabinets. Also do not eat raw or partly cooked meats, pâté, unpasteurised milk or soil-dirty fruits and vegetables, as they can cause toxoplasmosis.

∞ Meat and fish – Certain meats and poultry carry the potential risk of salmonella and should be cooked thoroughly until the juices run clear and there is no pinkness left.

Pay particular attention when buying and cooking fish. Buy only the freshest, which should smell salty but not strong or fishy. Look for bright eyes and reject any with sunken eyes. The bodies should look fresh, plump and shiny, not dry, shrivelled or damp.

It is best to avoid any shellfish while pregnant, unless it is definitely fresh and thoroughly cooked, as it may contain harmful bacteria and viruses.

Later Life

There is evidence that the immune system becomes weaker as we get older, which can increase the risk of cancer and other illnesses. Maintaining a diet rich in antioxidants, fresh fruits and vegetables, plant oils and oily fish is especially beneficial in order to either prevent these illnesses or minimise their effects. As with all age groups, the body benefits from the five-a-day plan – to eat five portions of fruit or vegetables each day. Leafy green vegetables such as cabbage, broccoli, Brussels sprouts, cauliflower and kale are rich in antioxidants, which lower the risk of cancer.

Foods which are green in colour tend to provide nutrients essential for healthy nerves, muscles and hormones, while foods red in colour protect against cardiovascular disease. Other foods which can also assist in preventing cardiovascular disease and ensuring a healthy heart include vitamins E and C, oily fish and essential fats (such as extra virgin olive oil and garlic). They help lower blood cholesterol levels and clear arteries. A diet high in fresh fruits and vegetables and low in salt and saturated fats can considerably reduce heart disease.

Other foods have recognised properties. Certain types of mushrooms are known to boost the immune system, while garlic not only boosts the immune system, but also protects the body against cancer. Live yogurt too, has healthy properties, as it contains gut-friendly bacteria which help digestion. Some foods, such as soya can help to regulate the body's hormone levels during the menopause. Studies have shown that a regular intake of soya can help to protect the body against breast and prostate cancer.

Store-cupboard Essentials

L ow-fat cooking has often been associated with the stigma that reducing fat reduces flavour. This simply is not the case, which is great news for those choosing a lower-fat diet. Modern lifestyles are naturally shifting towards lower-fat and cholesterol diets, so there is no need to compromise on the choice of foods we eat, thanks to the increasing number of lower-fat products now available on the high street.

The store cupboard is a good place to start when cooking low-fat meals. Most of us have fairly limited cooking and preparation time available during the week, so choose to experiment during weekends. When time is of the essence, or friends arrive unannounced, it is always a good idea, especially when following a low-fat diet, to have some well thought-out basics in the cupboard, that is, foods that are high in flavour and low in fat.

As store-cupboard ingredients keep reasonably well, it really is worth making a trip to a good speciality grocery shop. Our society's growing obsession in recent years with travel and food from around the world has led us to seek out alternative ingredients with which to experiment and incorporate into our cooking.

Consequently, supermarket chains have had to broaden their product range and often have a specialist range of imported ingredients from around the world.

If the grocer or local supermarket only carries a limited choice of products, do not despair. The internet now offers freedom to the food shopaholics amongst us. There are some fantastic food sites (both local and international) where food can be purchased and delivery arranged online. When thinking about essentials, think of flavour, something that is going to add to a dish without increasing its fat content. It is worth spending a little bit more money on these products, to make flavoursome dishes that will help stop the urge to snack on fatty foods.

Store-cupboard Hints

There are many different types of store-cupboard ingredients which are readily available – including myriad varieties of rice and pasta – which are very versatile and can provide much of the carbohydrate required in our daily diets. Store the ingredients in a cool, dark place and remember to rotate the store-cupboard ingredients occasionally. By following these guidelines, the ingredients will be safe to use for approximately six months.

- Bulgur wheat – A cracked wheat which is often used in tabbouleh. Bulgur wheat is a good source of complex carbohydrate.

- Couscous – Now available in instant form, couscous just needs to be covered with boiling water, then forked. Couscous is a precooked wheat semolina. Traditional couscous needs to be steamed and is available from health food stores. This type of couscous contains more nutrients than the instant variety.

- Dried fruit – The ready-to-eat varieties are particularly good, as they are plump, juicy and do not need to be soaked. They are fantastic when puréed into a compote, added to water and heated to make a pie filling and when added to stuffing mixtures. They are also good cooked with meats, rice or couscous.

- Flours – A useful addition (particularly cornflour), which can be used to thicken sauces. It is worth mentioning that wholegrain flour should not be stored for too long at room temperature, as the fats may turn rancid. While not strictly a flour, cornmeal is a very versatile low-fat ingredient, which can be used when making dumplings and gnocchi.

- Noodles – Noodles are also very useful and can accompany any Far-Eastern dish. They are low-fat and also available in the wholewheat variety. Rice noodles are available for those who have gluten-free diets and, like pasta noodles, provide slow-release energy to the body.

- **Pasta** – It is good to have a mixture of wholewheat and plain pasta as well as a wide variety of flavoured pastas. Whether fresh (it can also be frozen) or dried, pasta is a versatile ingredient with which to provide the body with slow-release energy. It comes in many different sizes and shapes; from the tiny tubettini (which can be added to soups to create a more substantial dish), to penne, fusilli, rigatoni and conchiglie, up to the larger cannelloni and lasagne sheets.

- **Pot and pearl barley** – Pot barley is the complete barley grain, whereas pearl barley has the outer husk removed. A high-cereal diet can help to prevent bowel disorders and diseases.

- **Pulses** – A vital ingredient for the store cupboard, they are easy to store, have a very high nutritional value and are great when added to soups, casseroles, curries and hotpots. Pulses also act as a thickener, whether flavoured or on their own. They come in two forms: either dried (in which case, they generally need to be soaked overnight and then cooked before use – it is important to follow the instructions on the back of the packet), or canned, which is a convenient time-saver, because the preparation of dried pulses can take a while. If buying canned pulses, try to buy the variety in water with no added salt or sugar. These simply need to be drained and rinsed before being added to a dish.

Kidney beans, borlotti, cannellini, butter, flageolet beans, split peas and lentils all make tasty additions to any dish. Baked beans are a favourite with everyone and many shops now stock the organic variety, which have no added salt or sugar but are sweetened with fruit juice instead.

When boiling previously dried pulses, remember that salt should not be added, as this will make the skins tough and inedible. Puy lentils are a smaller variety. They often have mottled skins and are particularly good for cooking in slow dishes, as they hold their shape and firm texture particularly well.

- **Rice** – Basmati and Thai fragrant rice are well-suited to Thai and Indian curries, as the fine grains absorb the sauce and their delicate creaminess balances the pungency of the spices.

Arborio is only one type of risotto rice. Many are available, depending on whether the risotto is meant to accompany meat, fish or vegetable dishes. When cooked, rice swells to create a substantial low-fat dish. Easy-cook American rice, both plain and wholegrain, is great for casseroles and for stuffing meat, fish and vegetables, as it holds its shape and firmness. Pudding rice can be used in a variety of ways to create an irresistible dessert.

∾ Stock – Good-quality stock is a must in low-fat cooking, as it provides a good flavour base for many dishes. Many supermarkets now carry a variety of fresh and organic stocks, which although they need refrigeration, are probably one of the most time- and effort-saving ingredients available. There is also a fairly large range of dried stocks, perhaps the best being bouillon, a high-quality form of stock (available in powder or liquid form) which can be added to any dish, whether it be a sauce, casserole, pie or soup.

∾ Other sauces and flavourings – Many people favour meals which can be prepared and cooked in 30–45 minutes, so helpful ingredients which kick-start a sauce are great. A good-quality passata or canned plum tomatoes can act as the foundation for any sauce, as can a good-quality green or red pesto. Other handy store-cupboard essentials include tapenade, mustard and anchovies. These ingredients have very distinctive tastes and are particularly flavoursome. Roasted red pepper sauce and sun-dried tomato purée, which tends to be sweeter and more intensely flavoured than regular tomato purée, are also very useful.

Vinegar is another worthwhile store-cupboard essential and with so many uses, it is worth splashing out on a really good-quality balsamic and wine vinegar. Herbs and spices are a must too. Using herbs when cooking at home should reduce the temptation to buy ready-made sauces. Often, these types of sauces contain large amounts of sugar and additives.

Yeast extract is also a good store-cupboard ingredient. It can pep up sauces, soups and casseroles and adds a little substance, particularly to vegetarian dishes. Eastern flavours offer a lot of scope where low-fat cooking is concerned. Flavourings such as fish sauce, soy sauce, red and green curry paste and Chinese rice wine all add mouthwatering, low-fat flavours to any dish.

Guilt-free

Salads

Perhaps one of the most renowned 'guilt-free' foods, salads have a lot to offer for those hoping to lose weight and lead a healthier lifestyle. Packed with vegetables, fruits and low-fat proteins such as fish, tofu and nuts, this chapter showcases some of the healthiest salads around, without compromising on taste. For satisfaction without the calories, try Sugar Snap Pea and Roasted Hazelnut Salad, or for a sophisticated lunch, the Smoked Trout & Grilled Peach Salad is a must-try!

Greek Salad

Serves 4

1 medium red onion
$1/2$ cucumber
4 ripe medium tomatoes
175 g/6 oz feta cheese
50 g/2 oz Kalamata olives or large
black olives, preferably pitted
2–3 lemon thyme sprigs
2 tbsp low-fat Greek extra virgin
olive oil

Health Tip

Using olive oil, especially extra
virgin olive oil, is extremely good
for you, as it helps to boost the
immune system and to protect
the body against viruses. It is
also reputed to help in the fight
against various diseases, such as
cancer and heart disease.

Peel the onion and cut in half, then cut in half again and slice
thinly to form half moons. Reserve.

Peel the cucumber and cut into small pieces. Rinse the
tomatoes and cut into wedges and reserve both.

Drain the cheese and cut into small cubes.

Mix all the prepared ingredients together in a large bowl, then
divide between four individual bowls or plates. Arrange the
olives on top. Shred a little of the lemon thyme over and drizzle
with the olive oil. Garnish with the remaining thyme and serve.

Rice Papaya Salad

Serves 4

175 g/6 oz easy-cook basmati rice
1 cinnamon stick, bruised
zest and juice of 2 limes
1 bird's-eye chilli, deseeded and
finely chopped
zest and juice of 2 lemons
2 tbsp Thai fish sauce
1 tbsp soft light brown sugar
1 papaya, peeled and
seeds removed
1 mango, peeled and
stone removed
1 green chilli, deseeded and
finely chopped
2 tbsp freshly chopped coriander
1 tbsp freshly chopped mint
250 g/9 oz cooked chicken
50 g/2 oz roasted peanuts, chopped
pitta bread strips, to serve

Rinse and drain the rice and pour into a saucepan. Add 450 ml/³/₄ pint boiling salted water and the cinnamon stick. Bring to the boil, reduce to a very low heat, cover and cook without stirring for 15–18 minutes until all the liquid is absorbed. The rice should be light and fluffy and have steam holes on the surface. Remove the cinnamon stick and stir in the zest from one lime.

To make the dressing, place the bird's-eye chilli, remaining zest and lime and lemon juice and zest, fish sauce and sugar in a food processor, mix for a few minutes until blended. Alternatively, place all these ingredients in a screw-top jar and shake until well blended. Pour half the dressing over the hot rice and toss until the rice glistens.

Slice the papaya and mango into thin slices, then place in a bowl. Add the chopped green chilli, coriander and mint. Place the chicken on a chopping board, then remove and discard any skin or sinew. Cut into fine shreds and add to the bowl with the chopped peanuts.

Add the remaining dressing to the chicken mixture and stir until all the ingredients are lightly coated. Spoon the rice onto a platter, pile the chicken mixture on top and serve with warm strips of pitta bread.

Grilled Pumpkin Salad with Feta Pine Nuts

Serves 4

450 g/1 lb pumpkin
1 tbsp olive oil
50 g/2 oz pine nuts
175 g/6 oz feta cheese
75 g/3 oz rocket
50 g/2 oz black olives,
preferably pitted
2 tbsp extra virgin olive oil

Peel the pumpkin, discard the seeds and cut the flesh into small cubes. Bring a pan of water to the boil, then add the pumpkin, reduce the heat to a gentle simmer and cook for 15 minutes, or until tender. Drain.

Line a grill rack with kitchen foil and preheat the grill to medium. Place the drained pumpkin on the lined rack and drizzle with the oil. Place under the grill and cook for 10 minutes, or until lightly browned. Reserve.

Spread the pine nuts on the lined grill pan and grill for 1–2 minutes until golden, stirring frequently and making sure that they do not burn. Remove from the heat and allow to cool. Drain the feta, then cut into small cubes. Reserve.

Rinse the rocket, drain, then place in a serving bowl. Top with the pumpkin, pine nuts, feta and olives. Drizzle the oil over the top or hand around separately and serve.

Seared Scallop Salad

Serves 4

12 king (large) scallops
1 tbsp low-fat spread or butter
2 tbsp orange juice
2 tbsp balsamic vinegar
1 tbsp clear honey
2 ripe pears, washed
125 g/4 oz rocket
125 g/4 oz watercress
50 g/2 oz walnuts
freshly ground black pepper

Clean the scallops, removing the thin black vein from around the white meat and coral. Rinse thoroughly and dry on absorbent kitchen paper.

Cut into 2–3 thick slices, depending on the scallop size.

Heat a griddle pan or heavy-based frying pan, then, when hot, add the low-fat spread or butter and allow to melt.

Once melted, sear the scallops for 1 minute on each side, or until golden. Remove from the pan and reserve.

Briskly whisk together the orange juice, balsamic vinegar and honey to make the dressing and reserve.

With a small, sharp knife, carefully cut the pears into quarters, core, then cut into chunks.

Mix the rocket leaves, watercress, pear chunks and walnuts. Pile onto serving plates and top with the scallops. Drizzle over the dressing and grind over plenty of black pepper. Serve immediately.

Sugar Snap Pea and Roasted Hazelnut Salad

Serves 4

50 g/2 oz shelled hazelnuts
1 medium onion
175 g/6 oz sugar snap peas
2 tbsp basil olive oil
freshly ground black pepper

Preheat the oven to 190°C/375°F/Gas Mark 5, 10 minutes before cooking.

Place the nuts on a baking tray and cook in the oven for 8–10 minutes until golden, stirring at least twice during cooking. Remove and allow to cool. Alternatively, grill according to the instructions on page 36.

Peel the onion, cut in half, give a half turn and slice forming half moon shapes, then reserve.

Trim the sugar snap peas and cook them in a pan of boiling salted water for 3–4 minutes until just cooked and they still have a crunch. Drain, plunge into cold water to stop the cooking process, then drain again. Cut any large sugar snaps in half or quarters.

Place the sugar snaps in a bowl, add the onion and roasted nuts together with the oil and black pepper to taste. Toss together, then spoon into a serving dish and serve.

Bulgur Wheat Salad with Minty Lemon Dressing

Serves 4

125 g/4 oz bulgur wheat
10 cm /4 in piece cucumber
2 shallots, peeled
125 g/4 oz baby sweetcorn
3 ripe but firm tomatoes

For the dressing:

grated zest of 1 lemon
3 tbsp lemon juice
3 tbsp freshly chopped mint
2 tbsp freshly chopped parsley
1–2 tsp clear honey
2 tbsp sunflower oil
salt and freshly ground
black pepper

Place the bulgur wheat in a saucepan and cover with boiling water.

Simmer for about 10 minutes, then drain thoroughly and turn into a serving bowl.

Cut the cucumber into small dice, chop the shallots finely and reserve. Steam the sweetcorn over a pan of boiling water for 10 minutes, or until tender. Drain and slice into thick chunks.

Cut a cross in the top of each tomato and place in boiling water until their skins start to peel away.

Remove the skins and the seeds and cut the tomatoes into small dice.

Make the dressing by briskly whisking all the ingredients in a small bowl until mixed well. When the bulgur wheat has cooled a little, add all the prepared vegetables and stir in the dressing. Season to taste with salt and pepper and serve.

Waldorf Salad

Serves 4

2–3 celery stalks
2 little gems or 1 cos lettuce
3 red eating apples
3 tbsp lemon juice
50 g/2 oz raisins
75 g/3 oz shelled walnuts
2 tbsp extra virgin olive oil

Health Tip

When using eating or dessert apples, try not to peel them, as the skin provides a good source of fibre.

Using a small, sharp knife, trim the celery, then remove any tough strands by making a small slit at the top of each stalk on the outside and pulling down. Repeat three or four times, then slice and reserve.

Discard the root from the lettuce and rinse lightly. Shake off the excess water and tear into pieces.

Rinse the apples and cut into quarters. Discard the cores then slice the apple quarters thinly. Place the lemon juice in a bowl, add the apples and stir until lightly coated. Reserve both the apples and the lemon juice.

Arrange the lettuce in a serving bowl and arrange the other ingredients, including the raisins and walnuts, on top. Mix the reserved lemon juice with the olive oil and pour over the salad. Serve.

Chinese Salad with Soy
Ginger Dressing

Serves 4

1 head Chinese cabbage
200 g can water chestnuts, drained
6 spring onions, trimmed
4 ripe but firm cherry tomatoes
125 g/4 oz mangetout
125 g/4 oz beansprouts
2 tbsp freshly chopped coriander

For the soy and ginger dressing:

2 tbsp sunflower oil
4 tbsp light soy sauce
2.5 cm/1 in piece root ginger, peeled and finely grated
zest and juice of 1 lemon
salt and freshly ground black pepper
crusty white bread, to serve

Rinse and finely shred the Chinese cabbage and place in a serving dish.

Slice the water chestnuts into small slivers and cut the spring onions diagonally into 2.5 cm/1 inch lengths, then split lengthways into thin strips.

Cut the tomatoes in half and then slice each half into three wedges and reserve.

Simmer the mangetout in boiling water for 2 minutes until beginning to soften, drain and cut in half diagonally.

Arrange the water chestnuts, spring onions, mangetout, tomatoes and beansprouts on top of the shredded Chinese cabbage. Garnish with the freshly chopped coriander.

Make the dressing by whisking all the ingredients together in a small bowl until thoroughly mixed. Serve with the bread and the salad.

Tofu Sesame Salad

Serves 4

2 tbsp sesame seeds
175 g/6 oz firm smoked tofu
2 tbsp olive oil
4 medium tomatoes
175 g/6 oz rocket

Health Tip

Tofu provides an excellent source of protein, so is especially good for vegetarians.

Heat a nonstick frying pan over a medium heat until hot, then sprinkle in the sesame seeds and cook, stirring with a wooden spatula, for 1 minute, or until golden. Remove from the heat and place in a small bowl. If preferred, the seeds can be toasted with the tofu.

Drain the tofu and cut into small cubes. Heat the oil in a frying pan and fry the tofu cubes for 2 minutes, stirring frequently. Sprinkle in the sesame seeds and continue to cook for a further 1–2 minutes until the tofu is golden.

Rinse the tomatoes, slice, then arrange around a serving dish. Place the rocket in the centre of the bowl and top with the tofu and sesame seeds. Serve warm.

Carrot, Celeriac Sesame Seed Salad

Serves 6

225 g/8 oz celeriac
225 g/8 oz carrots, peeled
50 g/2 oz seedless raisins
2 tbsp sesame seeds
freshly chopped parsley,
to garnish

For the lemon & chilli dressing:

grated zest of 1 lemon
4 tbsp lemon juice
2 tbsp sunflower oil
2 tbsp clear honey
1 red bird's-eye chilli, deseeded
and finely chopped
salt and freshly ground
black pepper

Slice the celeriac into thin matchsticks. Place in a small saucepan of boiling salted water and boil for 2 minutes.

Drain and rinse the celeriac in cold water and place in a mixing bowl.

Finely grate the carrot. Add the carrot and the raisins to the celeriac in the bowl.

Place the sesame seeds under a hot grill, or dry-fry in a frying pan, for 1–2 minutes until golden brown, then leave to cool.

Make the dressing by whisking together the lemon zest, lemon juice, oil, honey, chilli and seasoning, or by shaking thoroughly in a screw-top jar.

Pour 2 tablespoons of the dressing over the salad and toss well. Turn into a serving dish and sprinkle over the toasted sesame seeds and chopped parsley. Serve the remaining dressing separately.

Courgette Mozzarella Salad

Serves 4

350 g/12 oz large courgettes
pinch salt
1 lettuce, such as romaine, or baby
salad leaves
75 g/3 oz mozzarella cheese
2 tbsp basil-flavoured extra virgin
olive oil
pinch paprika
2–3 tsp finely chopped red chilli
freshly ground black pepper
few basil leaves (optional)

Trim both ends of the courgettes and, using a vegetable peeler, cut the courgettes into long, thin strips or ribbons. Bring a large saucepan of water to the boil and add the salt. Cook the courgettes in batches for 1 minute, removing each batch with a pair of tongs or a large spoon, and drain thoroughly in a colander.

Rinse the lettuce, tear into pieces and place in a serving dish. Arrange the courgette ribbons on top of the lettuce together with spoonfuls of the fresh mozzarella. Sprinkle with the basil-flavoured olive oil, the paprika, chopped chilli and black pepper to taste. Garnish with basil leaves, if liked, and serve.

Cucumber ❧ Celery Salad with a Dill ❧ Yogurt Dressing

Serves 4

1 large cucumber
pinch salt

For the dressing:

300 ml/¹/₂ pint low-fat Greek yogurt
1–2 garlic cloves
2 tbsp lemon juice
freshly ground black pepper
dill sprigs, to garnish

Healthy Tip

Greek yogurt, especially the low-fat variety, is one of the healthiest foods one can eat. Being low in saturated fat, it is very beneficial for the heart. It is a guilt-free food, ideal as a snack at any time and great if you are on a weight-loss programme.

Peel the cucumber, then slice thinly. Place in layers in a colander, sprinkling each layer with a little salt. Leave for 30 minutes, then rinse thoroughly and allow to drain well. If the cucumber is too wet, then dry on absorbent kitchen paper.

Meanwhile, place the yogurt, garlic, lemon juice and black pepper to taste in a food processor and whizz for 1–2 minutes until thoroughly blended.

Place the cucumber in a large bowl and carefully tip in the prepared dressing. Stir lightly until all the cucumber is well coated in the dressing, then spoon into a serving dish, garnish with dill and serve.

Beetroot Potato Medley

Serves 4

350 g/12 oz raw baby beetroot
$^1/_2$ tsp sunflower oil
225 g/8 oz new potatoes
$^1/_2$ cucumber, peeled
3 tbsp white wine vinegar
150 ml/5 fl oz natural low-fat yogurt
salt and freshly ground
black pepper
fresh salad leaves
1 tbsp freshly snipped chives,
to garnish

Preheat the oven to 180°C/350°F/Gas Mark 4. Scrub the beetroot thoroughly and place on a baking tray.

Brush the beetroot with a little oil and cook for 1$^1/_2$ hours, or until a skewer is easily inserted into the beetroot. Allow to cool a little, then remove the skins.

Cook the potatoes in boiling water for about 10 minutes. Rinse in cold water and drain. Reserve the potatoes until cool. Dice evenly.

Cut the cucumber into cubes and place in a mixing bowl. Chop the beetroot into small cubes and add to the bowl with the reserved potatoes. Gently mix the vegetables together.

Mix together the vinegar and yogurt and season to taste with a little salt and pepper. Pour over the vegetables and combine gently.

Arrange on a bed of salad leaves garnished with the snipped chives and serve.

Pumpkin Salad with Figs, Mushrooms & Grapes

Serves 4

450 g/1 lb piece pumpkin
2 slices white bread, at least
1 day old
50 g/2 oz button mushrooms
2 tbsp olive oil
125 g/4 oz small tomatoes
(not cherry tomatoes)
4 ripe figs
50 g/2 oz green seedless grapes
125–4/4 oz assorted salad leaves
1 tbsp snipped chives

For the dressing:

2 tbsp extra virgin olive oil
1 tbsp raspberry vinegar
1 tsp clear honey
freshly ground black pepper

Peel the pumpkin, discard the seeds and cut the flesh into small cubes. Bring a pan of water to the boil, then add the pumpkin, reduce the heat to a gentle simmer and cook for 15 minutes, or until tender. Drain and reserve.

Cut the bread into small cubes, then wipe the mushrooms with kitchen paper and slice. Heat 1 tablespoon of the oil in a nonstick frying pan, add the bread and fry, stirring, for 2–3 minutes until golden. Drain on absorbent kitchen paper and reserve.

Heat the remaining oil in a small saucepan and fry the mushrooms for 4–5 minutes until cooked. Drain on absorbent kitchen paper and reserve.

Rinse the tomatoes and figs and cut into quarters. Rinse the grapes and reserve.

Rinse the salad leaves and arrange in a serving dish, then place the prepared ingredients on top and scatter over the croutons.

Place all the dressing ingredients in a screw-top jar, cover with the lid and shake until blended. Pour over the salad and serve garnished with snipped chives.

French Bean Tomato Salad

Serves 4

350 g/12 oz French beans
225 g/8 oz small ripe tomatoes
(not cherry tomatoes)
a few flat-leaf parsley sprigs

For the dressing:

2 tbsp extra virgin olive oil
1 tbsp white wine vinegar
pinch salt
pinch soft light brown sugar
freshly ground black pepper
2 tsp snipped chives

Trim the beans, discarding both ends, and cut into 5 cm/2 inch pieces. Rinse lightly, then cook in a pan of lightly salted boiling water for 5 minutes, or until just tender. Drain and plunge into cold water to stop cooking, then drain again. Place in a serving dish.

Lightly rinse the tomatoes and cut into quarters, then add to the beans in the serving dish.

Place all the dressing ingredients in a screw-top jar, cover with the lid and shake vigorously until blended. Pour over the salad, toss lightly, then garnish with parsley before serving.

Panzanella

Serves 4

250 g/9 oz day-old Italian-style bread
1 tbsp red wine vinegar
4 tbsp olive oil
1 tsp lemon juice
1 small garlic clove, peeled and
finely chopped
1 red onion, peeled and finely sliced
1 cucumber, peeled if preferred
225 g/8 oz ripe tomatoes, deseeded
150 g/5 oz pitted black olives
about 20 basil leaves, coarsely torn,
or left whole if small
sea salt and freshly ground
black pepper

Cut the bread into thick slices, leaving the crusts on. Add 1 teaspoon of the red wine vinegar to a jug of iced water, put the slices of bread in a bowl and pour over the water. Make sure the bread is covered completely. Leave to soak for 3–4 minutes until just soft.

Remove the soaked bread from the water and squeeze it gently, first with your hands and then in a clean tea towel, to remove any excess water. Put the bread on a plate, cover with clingfilm and chill in the refrigerator for about 1 hour.

Meanwhile, whisk together the olive oil, the remaining red wine vinegar and lemon juice in a large serving bowl. Add the garlic and onion and stir to coat well.

Halve the cucumber and remove the seeds. Chop both the cucumber and tomatoes into 1 cm/^{1}/$_2$ inch dice. Add to the garlic and onions with the olives. Tear the bread into bite-size chunks and add to the bowl with the fresh basil leaves. Toss together to mix and serve immediately with a grinding of sea salt and black pepper.

Watermelon Salad with Feta Cheese and Olives

Serves 4

¹/₄ piece large watermelon
175 g/6 oz feta cheese
50 g/2 oz black olives,
preferably pitted
a few lemon verbena sprigs

For the dressing:

2 tbsp freshly squeezed lime or
lemon juice
pinch freshly ground black pepper
¹/₂ tsp grated nutmeg

Cut the watermelon away from the rind and discard the seeds. Cut the flesh into small cubes and put in a large bowl.

Drain any liquid from the feta and cut into cubes, then add to the watermelon together with the olives and toss lightly together before piling into a serving dish.

Place all the dressing ingredients in a screw-top jar, cover with the lid and shake until blended. Pour the dressing over the watermelon, then garnish with the lemon verbena and serve.

Mango Avocado Salad

Serves 4

4 small ripe avocados
1 tbsp lemon juice
1 large or 2 medium ripe mangoes
125 g/4 oz rocket
50 g/2 oz walnuts
finely grated Parmesan cheese,
to garnish

For the dressing:

3 tbsp white wine vinegar
1 tbsp extra virgin olive oil
pinch crushed chillies

Health Tip

Avocados, although high in calories,
can play an important part in your
diet. They are reputed to help in
the fight against heart disease
and diabetes as well as helping
weight loss, arthritis and to
improve the skin.

Cut the avocados in half, then remove and discard the stones. Peel, then cut into slices and brush with the lemon juice to prevent the flesh going brown.

Cut the mango away from the stone, then peel and cut into chunks. Add to the avocado.

Rinse the rocket, then place in a serving dish. Top with the avocado and mango. Sprinkle over the walnuts and toss lightly together.

Place all the dressing ingredients in a screw-top jar, cover with the lid and shake until well blended. Pour over the salad, garnish with finely grated Parmesan cheese and serve.

Strawberry, Baby Spinach and Feta Salad

Serves 4

225 g/8 oz ripe strawberries
175 g/6 oz feta cheese
175 g/6 oz baby spinach leaves
50 g/2 oz walnuts or pine nuts, or a
mixture of both

For the dressing:

pinch salt and freshly ground
black pepper
$^1/_2$ tsp clear honey, or to taste

Hull the strawberries, then rinse lightly and leave until dry. Slice in half and reserve.

Drain off the liquid from the feta and then cut into small pieces and reserve.

Rinse the spinach leaves and shake well to remove any excess water. Place in a serving dish and arrange the strawberries and on cheese top. Sprinkle with the nuts.

Place all the dressing ingredients in a screw-top jar, cover with the lid and shake well. Pour the dressing over the salad and serve.

Niçoise Salad

Serves 4

1 small iceberg lettuce
225 g/8 oz French beans
225 g/8 oz baby new potatoes,
scrubbed
4 medium eggs
1 green pepper
1 medium onion, peeled
200 g can tuna in brine, drained
and flaked into small pieces
50 g/2 oz low-fat hard cheese, such
as Edam, cut into small cubes
8 ripe but firm cherry tomatoes,
quartered
50 g/2 oz pitted black olives, halved
freshly chopped basil, to garnish

For the lime vinaigrette:

3 tbsp light olive oil
2 tbsp white wine vinegar
4 tbsp lime juice
grated zest of 1 lime
1 tsp Dijon mustard
1–2 tsp caster sugar
salt and freshly ground black pepper

Cut the lettuce into quarters and remove the hard core. Tear into bite-size pieces and arrange on a large serving platter or four individual plates.

Cook the French beans in boiling salted water for 8 minutes and the potatoes for 10 minutes, or until tender. Drain and rinse in cold water until cool, then cut both the beans and potatoes in half with a sharp knife.

Boil the eggs for 10 minutes, then rinse under cold running water until cool. Remove the shells under water and cut each egg into quarters.

Remove the seeds from the pepper and cut into thin strips and finely chop the onion.

Arrange the beans, potatoes, eggs, peppers and onion on top of the lettuce. Add the tuna, cheese and tomatoes. Sprinkle over the olives and garnish with the basil.

To make the vinaigrette, place all the ingredients in a screw-top jar and shake vigorously until everything is mixed thoroughly. Spoon 4 tablespoons over the top of the prepared salad and serve the remainder separately.

Grilled Salmon Caesar Salad with Seeded Crackers

Serves 4

4 small salmon fillets, each about
125 g/4 oz in weight
4 tbsp orange juice
freshly ground black pepper
1 small cos or romaine lettuce

For the dressing:

1 garlic clove
2 anchovy fillets
5 tbsp low-fat mayonnaise

To serve:

Parmesan cheese, finely grated
or shaved (optional)
lemon wedges
seeded crackers

Remove and discard any pin bones from the salmon fillets and rinse lightly. Place in a shallow dish, pour over the orange juice and season with pepper. Leave for 30 minutes.

Line a grill rack with kitchen foil and preheat the grill to medium. Remove the salmon from the orange juice and place skin-side up on the lined grill rack. Cook for 5 minutes, then turn over and continue to grill for 3–4 minutes until the salmon is cooked. Remove from the grill and leave for 5 minutes before discarding the skin and flaking the flesh into small pieces.

Meanwhile, rinse the lettuce, tear into pieces and place in a serving bowl or plate. Top with the salmon once cool.

Make the dressing by crushing the garlic and anchovy fillets together in a bowl, then stirring with black pepper, if liked, into the mayonnaise. Stir well and serve with the salad together with some Parmesan cheese, if liked, lemon wedges and seeded crackers.

Curly Endive Seafood Salad

Serves 4

1 head curly endive lettuce
2 green peppers
12.5 cm/5 inch piece cucumber
125 g/4 oz squid, cleaned and cut
into thin rings
225 g/8 oz baby asparagus spears
125 g/4 oz smoked salmon slices,
cut into wide strips
175 g/6 oz fresh cooked mussels
in their shells

For the lemon dressing:
2 tbsp sunflower oil
1 tbsp white wine vinegar
5 tbsp fresh lemon juice
1–2 tsp caster sugar
1 tsp mild wholegrain mustard
salt and freshly ground
black pepper

To garnish:
lemon slices
fresh coriander sprigs

Rinse and tear the endive into small pieces and arrange on a serving platter.

Remove the seeds from the peppers and cut the peppers and the cucumber into small dice. Sprinkle over the endive.

Bring a saucepan of water to the boil and add the squid rings. Bring back to the boil, then switch off the heat and leave it to stand for 5 minutes, then drain and rinse thoroughly in cold water.

Cook the asparagus in boiling water for 5 minutes, or until tender but just crisp. Arrange with the squid, smoked salmon and mussels on top of the salad.

To make the lemon dressing, put all the ingredients into a screw-top jar or into a small bowl and mix thoroughly until the ingredients are combined.

Spoon 3 tablespoons of the dressing over the salad and serve the remainder in a small jug. Garnish the salad with slices of lemon and sprigs of coriander and serve.

Smoked Trout Grilled Peach Salad

Serves 4

4 ripe peaches
1 tsp olive oil
4 smoked trout fillets
125 g/4 oz assorted salad leaves

For the dressing:

3 tbsp peach or orange juice
1 tbsp extra virgin olive oil

Health Tip

Oily fish, such as trout and salmon, are extremely good for the heart, as they contain a good amount of Omega-3 fatty acids, which are vital for maintaining a healthy life. Doctors recommend that oily fish should be eaten at least three times a week.

Line the grill rack with kitchen foil and preheat the grill. Cut the peaches in half and remove the stones. When the grill is hot, brush the peach halves with a little oil and place on the grill rack. Cook for 2–3 minutes until the peaches are lightly browned and warm. Reserve.

Flake the trout into small pieces and reserve.

Rinse the salad leaves and place in a serving bowl or platter, then top with the peaches and trout.

Place the dressing ingredients in a screw-top jar, cover with the lid and shake well. Pour over the salad and serve.

Fruit Salad

Serves 4

125 g/4 oz caster sugar
3 oranges
700 g/1½ lb lychees, peeled
and stoned
1 small mango
1 small pineapple
1 papaya
4 pieces stem ginger in syrup
4 tbsp stem ginger syrup
125 g/4 oz Cape gooseberries
125 g/4 oz strawberries, hulled
½ tsp almond extract

To decorate:

lime zest
mint leaves

Place the sugar and 300 ml/½ pint water in a small pan and heat, stirring gently until the sugar has dissolved. Bring to the boil and simmer for 2 minutes. Once a syrup has formed, remove from the heat and allow to cool.

Using a sharp knife, cut away the skin from the oranges, then slice thickly. Cut each slice in half and place in a serving dish with the syrup and lychees. Cut the mango lengthways along each side of the stone. To remove the flesh from the skin, score each half lengthways and widthways, then cut away the flesh from the skin to make bite-size pieces. Alternatively, peel the mango, then cut into thick slices around each side of the stone before cutting into bite-size pieces. Discard the stone and add the pieces to the syrup.

Using a sharp knife, carefully cut away the skin from the pineapple. Remove the central core using the knife or an apple corer, then cut the pineapple into segments and add to the syrup. Peel the papaya, then cut in half and remove the seeds. Cut the flesh into chunks, slice the ginger into matchsticks and add with the ginger syrup to the fruit in the syrup. Prepare the Cape gooseberries by removing the thin, papery skins and rinsing lightly.

Halve the strawberries, add to the fruit with the almond essence and chill for 30 minutes. Scatter with mint leaves and lime zest and serve.

Meat & Poultry

Adding some tasty meat or poultry to a salad is a great way to make it more filling and thus suffice as a meal in itself, rather than a starter or side. Covering beef, lamb, duck, chicken, turkey and more, this chapter features a tempting range of protein-rich salads. From classics such as Caesar Salad with Chicken to the more adventurous Bulgur Wheat, Liver and Clementine Salad, there is something to suit every taste.

Thai Beef Chilli Salad

Serves 4

1–2 red chillies
1 green chilli
small piece fresh root ginger
1 lemongrass stalk
1 medium red onion
1 small green papaya
1 red pepper
2 small courgettes
4 small bunches pak choi
400 g/14 oz beef steak
2 tbsp peanut or vegetable oil
125 g/4 oz beansprouts
sweet chilli sauce, to taste
lemon balm sprigs, to garnish

Cut the chillies in half and discard the seeds and membrane if preferred, then chop into small pieces. Grate the fresh ginger and, using a mallet or rolling pin, lightly bash the lemongrass stalk.

Peel the red onion and cut in half, then slice thinly and reserve. Peel the green papaya, remove the seeds with a teaspoon and cut the flesh into thin slices, then reserve.

Cut the red pepper into quarters and discard the seeds and membrane, then slice thinly. Trim the courgettes, cut in half, then cut into small pieces. Shred the pak choi and cut the beef into thin slices. Reserve.

Heat a wok, then add the oil and swirl the wok until the sides are lightly coated with the oil. Add the chillies, ginger and lemongrass and stir-fry for 30 seconds, then add the beef and stir-fry for 2 minutes.

Add the remaining vegetables except for the beansprouts and stir-fry for 1–2 minutes until the beef is cooked.

Add sweet chilli sauce to taste together with the beansprouts and continue to stir-fry for a further minute. Serve warm or cold, garnished with lemon balm.

Israeli Couscous Steak Salad

Serves 4

150 g/5 oz Israeli couscous
1 medium red onion
$^1/_2$ cucumber
125 g/4 oz assorted salad leaves
125 g/4 oz cherry tomatoes, rinsed
and halved
4 beef steaks, such as flank, sirloin
or rump, about 125 g/4 oz each
in weight

For the dressing:

1 tsp mustard
1 tbsp red wine vinegar
2 tbsp extra virgin olive oil

Place the couscous in a bowl and pour over boiling water to cover. Leave for 10 minutes, or until fluffy and the water has been absorbed. Using a fork, stir the couscous until the grains have been separated and are fluffy, then spoon into a serving dish.

Peel the onion and finely chop. Peel the cucumber and discard the seeds if preferred, then cut into small cubes.

Rinse the salad leaves and add to the couscous with the tomatoes and stir lightly.

Line a grill rack with kitchen foil and preheat the grill to medium. Place the steaks on the lined rack and cook for 2–3 minutes on each side, or until cooked to personal preference.

Meanwhile, place all the dressing ingredients in a screw-top jar, cover with the lid and shake until blended. Pour over the salad, then top with the cooked steak and serve.

Brown Rice & Lentil Salad with Duck

Serves 6

225 g/8 oz Puy lentils, rinsed; 4 tbsp olive oil; 1 medium onion, peeled and chopped; 200 g/7 oz long-grain brown rice; $^1/_2$ tsp dried thyme; 450 ml/$^3/_4$ pint chicken stock; salt and freshly ground black pepper; 350 g/12 oz shiitake or portabello mushrooms, trimmed and sliced; 375 g/13 oz cooked Chinese-style roasted duck, sliced; 2 garlic cloves, peeled and chopped; 125 g/4 oz cooked smoked ham, diced; 2 small courgettes, trimmed, diced and blanched; 6 spring onions, trimmed and thinly sliced; 2 tbsp freshly chopped parsley; 2 tbsp walnut halves, toasted and chopped

For the dressing:

2 tbsp red or white wine vinegar
1 tbsp balsamic vinegar
1 tsp Dijon mustard
1 tsp clear honey
75 ml/3 fl oz extra virgin olive oil
2–3 tbsp walnut oil

Bring a large saucepan of water to the boil, sprinkle in the lentils, return to the boil, then simmer over a low heat for 30 minutes, or until tender; do not overcook. Drain and rinse under cold running water, then drain again and reserve.

Heat 2 tablespoons of the oil in a saucepan. Add the onion and cook for 2 minutes until it begins to soften. Stir in the rice with the thyme and stock. Season to taste with salt and pepper and bring to the boil. Cover and simmer for 40 minutes, or until tender and the liquid is absorbed.

Heat the remaining oil in a large frying pan and add the mushrooms. Cook for 5 minutes until golden. Stir in the duck and garlic and cook for 2–3 minutes to heat through. Season well.

To make the dressing, whisk the vinegars, mustard and honey in a large serving bowl, then gradually whisk in the oils. Add the lentils and the rice, then stir lightly together. Gently stir in the ham, blanched courgettes, spring onions and parsley. Season to taste and sprinkle with the walnuts. Serve topped with the duck and mushrooms.

Grilled Lamb Fillet Salad with Parmesan Crisps

Serves 4

450 g/1 lb lamb fillet
3 tbsp olive oil
3 tbsp orange juice
1 tsp clear honey
salt and freshly ground
black pepper
1 small aubergine
175 g/6 oz French beans
8 cherry tomatoes
125 g/4 oz assorted salad leaves
extra virgin olive oil, for drizzling
2 spring onions, trimmed and
snipped, to garnish
bought Parmesan crisps, to serve

Cut the lamb into long, thin strips and place in a shallow dish. Blend 2 tablespoons of the oil with the orange juice and honey. Add seasoning to taste and pour over the lamb. Cover and leave to marinate in the refrigerator for at least 30 minutes.

Line a grill rack with kitchen foil and preheat the grill to medium. Cut the aubergine into thin strips or ribbons with a vegetable peeler, then brush lightly with the remaining oil. Place on the lined grill rack and grill until lightly golden and cooked. Remove from the rack and allow to cool.

Trim the French beans and cook in lightly salted boiling water for 4–5 minutes until just tender. Drain and plunge into cold water and drain again.

Rinse the tomatoes and salad leaves, cut the tomatoes in half and arrange with the salad leaves in a serving dish.

When ready to serve, line a grill rack with kitchen foil and preheat the grill to medium. Drain the lamb fillets and cook under the grill for 10–12 minutes until cooked to personal preference. Turn over at least three times during cooking. Remove from the heat and cut into smaller strips. Place on top of the salad, garnish with the spring onions and serve drizzled with oil and Parmesan crisps.

Caesar Salad with Chicken

Serves 4

2 slices white bread, at least
1 day old
2–3 tbsp olive oil
4 small skinless, boneless chicken
breast fillets, each about
125 g/4 oz in weight
1 cos or romaine lettuce
2 tbsp finely grated Parmesan
cheese, to serve

For the dressing:

1 large egg
1 garlic clove, peeled and crushed
2 anchovy fillets
2 tbsp lemon juice

Cut the bread into small squares. Heat 1 tablespoon of the oil in a nonstick frying pan. Add the bread and fry, stirring frequently, for 3–4 minutes until the bread is golden and crisp. Drain on absorbent kitchen paper and reserve.

Line a grill rack with kitchen foil and preheat the grill to medium. Rinse the chicken lightly and pat dry. Brush with the remaining oil and grill under a medium heat for 15–20 minutes until cooked and the juices run clear when pierced with a sharp knife. Turn over at least once during cooking. Remove from the grill and leave for 5 minutes before cutting into small pieces.

Meanwhile, rinse the lettuce, tear into pieces and place in a serving bowl or plate and top with the chicken once cool.

Make the dressing by whizzing all the ingredients together, then pour over the salad. Serve the salad sprinkled with the croutons and grated Parmesan cheese.

Chef's Rice Salad

Serves 4

225 g/8 oz wild rice
$^1/_2$ cucumber
175 g/6 oz cherry tomatoes
6 spring onions, trimmed
5 tbsp extra virgin olive oil
2 tbsp balsamic vinegar
1 tsp Dijon mustard
1 tsp caster sugar
salt and freshly ground black pepper
125 g/4 oz rocket
125 g/4 oz back bacon
125 g/4 oz cooked chicken meat, finely diced
125 g/4 oz Emmenthal cheese, grated
125 g/4 oz large cooked prawns, peeled
1 avocado, stoned, peeled and sliced, to garnish
warm crusty bread, to serve

Put the rice in a saucepan of water and bring to the boil, stirring once or twice. Reduce the heat, cover and simmer gently for 30–50 minutes, depending on the texture you prefer. Drain well and reserve.

Thinly peel the cucumber, cut in half, then, using a teaspoon, remove the seeds. Cut the cucumber into thin slices. Cut the tomatoes into quarters. Cut the spring onions into diagonal slices.

Whisk the olive oil with the vinegar, then whisk in the mustard and sugar. Season to taste with salt and pepper.

In a large bowl, gently toss together the cooled rice with the tomatoes, cucumber, spring onions and the rocket. Pour over the dressing and toss lightly together.

Heat a griddle pan and, when hot, cook the bacon on both sides for 4–6 minutes until crisp. Remove and chop. Arrange the prepared rocket salad on a platter, then arrange the bacon, chicken, cheese and prawns on top. Toss, if wished. Garnish with avocado slices and serve with plenty of warm crusty bread.

Apple & Cranberry Chicken Salad

Serves 4

4 skinless, boneless chicken breast fillets
2 tsp clear honey
1 tbsp olive oil
2 tbsp apple juice
salt and freshly ground black pepper
125 g/4 oz assorted salad leaves
50 g/2 oz dried cranberries
1 tbsp extra virgin olive oil
1–2 green eating apples, depending on size
1 tbsp finely grated mature Cheddar cheese (optional)

To serve:

lemon wedges
toasted ciabatta bread

Preheat the oven to 190°C/375°F/Gas Mark 5, 10 minutes before cooking.

Lightly rinse the chicken breasts and pat dry. Make four squares of kitchen foil large enough to encase the chicken, and place a chicken breast on each.

Stir the honey, olive oil and apple juice together and add seasoning to taste. Pour over the chicken, then fold the kitchen foil over to enclose the chicken completely. Place in a roasting tin and cook in the oven for 20 minutes. Fold back the kitchen foil and baste with the juices, then continue to cook for a further 10–15 minutes until the chicken is completely cooked and the juices run clear when each breast is pierced with a sharp knife. Reserve.

Meanwhile, rinse the salad leaves and place on four serving plates. Sprinkle over the cranberries and drizzle with a little extra virgin olive oil.

Rinse the apples, cut into quarters and discard the cores before cutting into slices. Make cuts in each chicken breast and place an apple slice in each cut, then sprinkle with the grated cheese, if using. Serve with lemon wedges and toasted ciabatta bread.

Chicken Pasta Salad

Serves 4

450 g/1 lb short pasta
2–3 tbsp extra virgin olive oil
300 g/11 oz cold cooked chicken,
cut into bite-size pieces
(preferably roasted)
1 red pepper, deseeded and diced
1 yellow pepper, deseeded
and diced
4–5 sun-dried tomatoes, sliced
2 tbsp capers, rinsed and drained
125 g/4 oz pitted Italian black olives
4 spring onions, chopped
225 g/8 oz mozzarella cheese,
preferably buffalo, diced
salt and freshly ground black pepper

For the dressing:

50 ml/2 fl oz red or white wine vinegar
1 tbsp mild mustard
1 tsp sugar
85–125 ml/3–4 fl oz extra virgin
olive oil
125 ml/4 fl oz mayonnaise

Bring a large saucepan of lightly salted water to the boil. Add the pasta and cook for 10 minutes, or until *al dente*.

Drain the pasta and rinse under cold running water, then drain again. Place in a large serving bowl and toss with the olive oil.

Add the chicken, diced red and yellow peppers, sliced sun-dried tomatoes, capers, olives, spring onions and mozzarella to the pasta and toss gently until mixed. Season to taste with salt and pepper.

To make the dressing, put the vinegar, mustard and sugar into a small bowl or jug and whisk until well blended and the sugar is dissolved. Season with some pepper, then gradually whisk in the olive oil in a slow, steady stream until a thickened vinaigrette forms.

Put the mayonnaise in a bowl and gradually whisk in the dressing until smooth. Pour over the pasta mixture and mix gently until all the ingredients are coated. Turn into a large, shallow serving bowl and serve at room temperature.

Chicken Salad Neapolitano

Serves 4

4 skinless, boneless chicken breasts
2 tbsp olive oil
salt and freshly ground
black pepper
a few tarragon sprigs
225 g/8 oz not new potatoes,
scrubbed and cut into small
wedges
125 g/4 oz assorted salad leaves
4 ripe tomatoes
50 g/2 oz Kalamata olives, pitted
and chopped
basil leaves, to garnish
2–3 tbsp low-fat natural Greek yogurt
or low-fat mayonnaise
1 tbsp snipped chives

Preheat the oven to 190°C/375°F/Gas Mark 5, 10 minutes before cooking.

Lightly rinse the chicken breasts and pat dry. Place in a roasting tin and pour over the olive oil and a little seasoning. Tuck some tarragon under the chicken and add the potato wedges. Roast in the oven for 20 minutes, then baste with oil and continue to roast for 10 minutes, or until the chicken and potatoes are cooked and the chicken juices run clear. Allow to cool, then cut into small pieces.

Rinse the salad leaves and shake off any excess water. Place on four individual serving plates. Rinse the tomatoes and cut into quarters. Arrange the tomatoes on the plates together with the olives, a few basil leaves and extra tarragon, if liked.

Arrange the chicken on top of the salad, then place small spoonfuls of yogurt or mayonnaise on top, sprinkle with the chives, garnish with basil and serve.

Turkey & Oven-roasted Vegetable Salad

Serves 4

6 tbsp olive oil

3 medium courgettes, trimmed and sliced

2 yellow peppers, deseeded and sliced

125 g/4 oz pine nuts

275 g/10 oz macaroni

350 g/12 oz cooked turkey

280 g jar or can chargrilled artichokes, drained and sliced

225 g/8 oz baby plum tomatoes, quartered

4 tbsp freshly chopped coriander

1 garlic clove, peeled and chopped

3 tbsp balsamic vinegar

salt and freshly ground black pepper

Preheat the oven to 200°C/400°F/Gas Mark 6, 15 minutes before cooking. Line a large roasting tin with foil, pour in half the olive oil and place in the oven for 3 minutes, or until very hot. Remove from the oven, add the courgettes and peppers and stir until evenly coated. Bake for 30–35 minutes until slightly charred, turning occasionally.

Add the pine nuts to the tin. Return to the oven and bake for 10 minutes, or until the pine nuts are toasted. Remove from the oven and allow the vegetables to cool completely.

Bring a large pan of lightly salted water to a rolling boil. Add the macaroni and cook according to the packet instructions, or until *al dente*. Drain and refresh under cold running water, then drain thoroughly and place in a large salad bowl.

Cut the turkey into bite-size pieces and add to the macaroni. Add the artichokes and tomatoes with the cooled vegetables and pan juices to the bowl. Blend together the coriander, garlic, remaining oil, vinegar and seasoning. Pour over the salad, toss lightly and serve.

Spicy Grilled Chicken and Couscous Salad

Serves 4

4 skinless, boneless chicken
breasts, each about 125 g/4 oz
in weight
1 tbsp sweet chilli sauce, or to taste
3 tbsp olive oil
175 g/6 oz couscous
about 600 ml/1 pint boiling chicken
stock or water
1 courgette
200 g/7 oz canned
chickpeas, drained
25 g/1 oz pine nuts,
toasted (optional)
1 tbsp freshly chopped parsley
1 ripe avocado
125 g/4 oz rocket
1 tbsp extra virgin olive oil,
for drizzling

Rinse the chicken and pat dry with kitchen paper. Place in a shallow dish.
Mix the chilli sauce with 2 tablespoons of the olive oil and pour over the
chicken. Cover with kitchen foil and leave in the refrigerator for 30
minutes, turning occasionally and basting with the chilli oil.

Place the couscous in a bowl and pour the boiling stock or water over.
Leave for 30 minutes, or until all the stock or water has been absorbed.
Fluff with a fork and reserve.

Line a grill rack with kitchen foil and preheat the grill to medium. Drain
the chicken and place on the lined grill rack. Cook for 20–25 minutes until
cooked and the juices run clear when pierced with a sharp knife. Remove
and allow to cool before cutting into small pieces. Reserve.

Meanwhile, trim the courgette and cut lengthways into quarters. Brush
lightly with the remaining olive oil, place under the grill and cook for
4–6 minutes until lightly charred.

Stir the courgette into the couscous together with the chicken, chickpeas,
pine nuts and chopped parsley. Cut the avocado in half, peel, stone, cut
into slices and stir into the salad. Rinse the rocket and pat dry, then stir
into the salad. Spoon into a serving dish and serve drizzled with the extra
virgin olive oil.

Spicy Chicken Pasta Salad

Serves 6

450 g/1 lb pasta shells
25 g/1 oz butter
1 onion, peeled and chopped
2 tbsp mild curry paste
125 g/4 oz ready-to-eat dried
apricots, chopped
2 tbsp tomato purée
3 tbsp mango chutney
300 ml/½ pint mayonnaise
425 g can pineapple slices
in fruit juice
salt and freshly ground black pepper
450 g/1 lb skinless, boneless
cooked chicken, cut into
bite-size pieces
25 g/1 oz flaked toasted
almond slivers
coriander sprigs, to garnish

Bring a large pan of lightly salted water to a rolling boil. Add the pasta shells and cook according to the packet instructions, or until *al dente*. Drain and refresh under cold running water, then drain thoroughly and place in a large serving bowl.

Meanwhile, melt the butter in a heavy-based pan, add the onion and cook for 5 minutes, or until softened. Add the curry paste and cook, stirring, for 2 minutes. Stir in the apricots and tomato purée, then cook for 1 minute. Remove from the heat and allow to cool.

Blend the mango chutney and mayonnaise together in a small bowl. Drain the pineapple slices, adding 2 tablespoons of the pineapple juice to the mayonnaise mixture; reserve the pineapple slices. Season the mayonnaise to taste with salt and pepper.

Cut the pineapple slices into chunks and stir into the pasta together with the mayonnaise mixture, curry mixture and cooked chicken pieces. Toss lightly together to coat the pasta. Sprinkle with the almond slivers, garnish with coriander sprigs and serve cold.

Chicken Satay Salad

Serves 4

4 tbsp crunchy peanut butter
1 tbsp chilli sauce
1 garlic clove, peeled and crushed
2 tbsp cider vinegar
2 tbsp light soy sauce
2 tbsp dark soy sauce
2 tsp soft brown sugar
pinch salt
2 tsp freshly ground Sichuan
peppercorns
450 g/1 lb dried egg noodles
2 tbsp sesame oil
1 tbsp groundnut oil
450 g/1 lb skinless, boneless chicken
breast fillets, cut into cubes
shredded celery leaves, to garnish
cos lettuce, to serve

Place the peanut butter, chilli sauce, garlic, cider vinegar, soy sauces, sugar, salt and ground peppercorns in a food processor and blend to form a smooth paste. Scrape into a bowl, cover and chill in the refrigerator until required.

Bring a large saucepan of lightly salted water to the boil. Add the noodles and cook for 3–5 minutes. Drain and plunge into cold water. Drain again and toss in the sesame oil and groundnut oil. Leave to cool.

Heat the wok until very hot, add the oil and, when hot, add the chicken cubes. Stir-fry for 5–6 minutes until the chicken is golden brown and cooked through.

Remove the chicken from the wok using a slotted spoon and add to the noodles together with the peanut sauce. Mix lightly together, then sprinkle with the shredded celery leaves and either serve immediately or leave until cold, then serve with cos lettuce.

Pear & Gorgonzola Salad with Proscuitto

Serves 4

6 ripe pears
1 tbsp lemon juice
125 g/4 oz rocket
175 g/6 oz Gorgonzola cheese
75 g/3 oz prosciutto
25 g/1 oz walnuts

For the dressing:

3 tbsp extra virgin olive oil
1 tbsp raspberry or other fruit-flavoured vinegar
freshly ground black pepper

Peel the pears, leaving the stalks intact, and remove the cores. Slice the pears thickly, brush with the lemon juice and reserve.

Lightly rinse the rocket and arrange on four individual serving plates or dishes. Cut the cheese into squares and layer with the pear slices on top of the rocket, as shown.

Line a grill rack with kitchen foil, and preheat the grill to medium. Arrange the prosciutto on the lined grill rack and cook for 1–2 minutes until warm and beginning to curl up at the edges. Remove and arrange with the pears. Scatter the walnuts over.

Place all the dressing ingredients in a screw-top jar, cover with the lid and shake well. Pour over the salad and serve.

Boiled Egg Bacon Salad

Serves 4

4 large eggs
225 g/8 oz back bacon rashers
125 g/4 oz baby button mushrooms
1 tbsp olive oil
125 g/4 oz baby spinach leaves,
washed
4 medium tomatoes,
washed and sliced
50 g/2 oz mature Cheddar cheese,
finely grated

For the dressing:

2 tbsp extra virgin olive oil
1 tbsp white wine vinegar
salt and freshly ground
black pepper
2–3 drops Worcestershire sauce

Place the eggs in a saucepan and cover with cold water. Bring to the boil, then reduce the heat to a simmer and cook for 10 minutes. Plunge immediately into cold water and leave until cold. When cold, peel and cut into slices. Do this just before using.

Line a grill rack with kitchen foil and preheat the grill to medium. Place the bacon on the lined grill rack and cook for 5–8 minutes until cooked, turning the bacon over at least once. Remove, chop into pieces and reserve.

Wipe the mushrooms with kitchen paper and trim the stalks. Heat the olive oil in a small saucepan and fry the mushrooms, stirring frequently, for 3–4 minutes until cooked. Drain and reserve.

Arrange all the prepared ingredients on a serving platter or individual plates and sprinkle with the cheese.

Place all the ingredients for the dressing in a screw-top jar, cover with the lid and shake vigorously until blended. Pour over the salad and serve.

Char Sui Pork Noodle Salad

Serves 4

200 g/7 oz flat rice noodles
4 tbsp black treacle
2 tbsp dark soy sauce
3 tbsp Chinese rice wine or
dry sherry
3 star anise, roughly crushed
1 cinnamon stick
350 g/12 oz pork tenderloin,
in one piece
1 tbsp groundnut oil
2 garlic cloves, peeled and
finely chopped
1 tsp freshly grated root ginger
3 spring onions, trimmed
and sliced
125 g/4 oz pak choi, roughly
chopped
2 tbsp light soy sauce
fresh coriander leaves, to garnish
prepared or bought plum sauce,
to serve

Preheat the oven to 220°C/425°F/Gas Mark 7, 15 minutes before cooking. Soak the noodles in boiling water, according to the packet instructions. Drain and reserve. Place the treacle, dark soy sauce, Chinese rice wine or sherry, star anise and cinnamon into a small saucepan and stir over a gentle heat until mixed thoroughly, then reserve.

Trim the pork tenderloin of any excess fat and put into a shallow dish. Pour the cooled sauce over the tenderloin. Turn the pork, making sure it is completely coated in the sauce. Place in the refrigerator and leave to marinate for 4 hours, turning occasionally.

Remove the pork from its marinade and transfer to a roasting tin. Roast in the preheated oven for 12–14 minutes, basting once, until the pork is cooked through. Remove from the oven and leave until just warm.

Heat the wok, add the oil and, when hot, add the garlic, ginger and spring onions. Stir-fry for 30 seconds before adding the pak choi. Stir-fry for a further 1 minute until the pak choi has wilted, then add the noodles and light soy sauce. Toss for a few seconds until well mixed, then transfer to a large serving dish. Leave to cool.

Thickly slice the pork fillet and add to the cooled noodles. Garnish with coriander leaves and serve with plum sauce.

Fig Prosciutto Salad

Serves 4

25 g/1 oz pine nuts
4 ripe figs
125 g/4 oz assorted salad leaves, or use rocket
125 g/4 oz prosciutto
2 small ripe peaches, cut into wedges
75 g/3 oz feta cheese

For the dressing:

1 tsp clear honey
$^{1}/_{2}$ tsp mustard powder
2 tbsp freshly squeezed lemon juice
2 tbsp extra virgin olive oil

Health Tip

When using olive oil, it is recommended that extra virgin olive oil is used only for pouring over as a dressing, as heating extra virgin olive oil will destroy the flavour. Use olive oil for cooking.

Heat a frying pan over a gentle heat and add the pine nuts. Cook, stirring, for 1–2 minutes until golden, taking care not to burn the nuts. Remove from the heat and reserve.

Lightly rinse the figs and cut into pieces. Rinse the salad leaves, shake off any excess water and arrange on four individual plates or in one large serving dish together with the prosciutto, figs and peach wedges.

Drain the feta cheese, then cut into small pieces and sprinkle over the salad together with the toasted pine nuts.

Place all the salad dressing ingredients in a screw-top jar, cover with the lid and shake well. Pour over the salad and serve.

Catalan Beans, Ham Chorizo

Serves 4

2 medium onions
450 g/1 lb lean bacon
85 ml/3 fl oz Spanish olive oil
125 g/4 oz chorizo
900 g/2 lb young broad beans
85 ml/3 fl oz Spanish white wine
1 bay leaf
sea salt and freshly ground
black pepper
1 tsp sugar, or to taste
150 ml/¼ pint mix anisette
and muscatel
fresh mint sprigs, to garnish

Peel and finely chop the onions. Roughly chop half the bacon. Heat the oil in a heavy-based saucepan, add the onions and fry for 3 minutes, then add the chopped bacon and cook for 5–8 minutes until golden, stirring frequently.

Slice the chorizo and add to the saucepan together with the broad beans. Stir well until lightly coated in the oil, then pour in the white wine and add the bay leaf.

Add the remaining bacon slices to the saucepan. Cover with a lid and simmer gently for 5 minutes. Add black pepper, sea salt and sugar to taste and continue to cook for 10 minutes, or until the beans are tender.

Pour in the anisette and muscatel mix, heat for 2–3 minutes, then serve garnished with a mint sprig.

Fig, Ham Cheese Salad

Serves 4

175 g/6 oz assorted salad leaves
125 g/4 oz thinly sliced
honey-roast ham
4 large or 8 small ripe figs
125 g/4 oz goat's cheese,
cut into cubes

For the dressing:

2 tbsp freshly squeezed
orange juice
1 tbsp extra virgin olive oil
salt and freshly ground black pepper

Health Tip

Goat's cheese is available as hard or
soft cheese and is readily found
in most supermarkets.
It makes a welcome change from
other cheeses and its distinctive
flavour combines well with many
different types of foods.

Lightly rinse the salad leaves, shake off the excess water and place in four individual serving bowls.

Cut each ham slice into strips, then roll up and reserve.

Rinse the figs and cut into pieces. Arrange all the prepared ingredients on top of the salad leaves together with the ham and cheese.

Place all the ingredients for the salad dressing in a screw-top jar, cover with the lid and shake well. Pour over the salad and serve.

Bulgur Wheat, Liver and Clementine Salad

Serves 4

175 g/6 oz bulgur wheat
350 ml/12 fl oz chicken stock or water
350 g/12 oz lamb's liver
1 tbsp plain flour
salt and freshly ground black pepper
125 g/4 oz assorted salad leaves
1–2 tbsp olive oil
4–6 clementines, depending on size
1 tbsp extra virgin olive oil
1 tbsp raisins
15 g/½ oz flaked almonds (optional)

Health Tip

Liver is an excellent source of protein as well as providing a high level of vitamins A D and E. Liver also has a high concentration of folic acid and iron. It is a good choice if following a low-fat diet or a weight-loss programme. Liver is classified as a 'superfood' and should be eaten on a regular basis.

Place the bulgur wheat in a bowl. Bring the chicken stock or water to the boil in a pan and pour over the bulgur wheat. Leave for 30 minutes, or until all the liquid has been absorbed, then stir with a fork to fluff up. Reserve.

Meanwhile, rinse the liver, discard any tubes or gristle and cut into small strips. Season the flour, then place in a bag with the liver. Seal or fold the bag over and shake until the liver is coated. Reserve. Lightly rinse the salad leaves and reserve.

Heat the olive oil in a frying pan and fry the liver for 4–6 minutes, stirring frequently, until the liver is cooked to personal preference. Drain on absorbent kitchen paper.

Peel the clementines and discard as much of the white pith as possible. Slice across the fruits and reserve.

When the bulgur wheat is ready, arrange the salad leaves on four serving plates. Stir the liver into the bulgur wheat, then spoon the mixture onto the plates. Drizzle with the extra virgin olive oil, add seasoning to taste, then add the clementines and raisins and serve garnished with flaked almonds, if using.

Fish & Seafood

Salads featuring fish and seafood are versatile, healthy and delicious. This chapter contains a host of original salad recipes based around a myriad of fish and seafoods including cod, mackerel, salmon, prawn and tuna. Why not tuck into a Poached Egg Salad with Smoked Salmon? Or for a tasty treat that is also visually striking, opt for the Prawn, Avocado & Mango Salad.

Red Pepper Cod Salad

Serves 4

225 g/8 oz salt cod
1 red pepper
1 Spanish onion
4 tbsp Spanish olive oil
1 tsp tomato purée
1 tbsp lemon juice
sea salt and freshly ground
black pepper
flat-leaf parsley sprigs, to garnish
toast, to serve

Soak the cod in enough cold water to cover for 24 hours, or longer if time permits. Leave covered in the refrigerator. When ready to use, drain and rinse. Place in a pan and cover with water. Poach for 8 minutes, or until tender. Drain and cool. When cool, remove and discard the skin and bones and divide into small chunks. Place in a bowl.

Preheat the grill and line the grill rack with kitchen foil. Cut the pepper into quarters and discard the seeds. Place the peppers skin-side up and grill for 10 minutes, or until charred. Turn the peppers round as necessary. Remove from the rack and place in a polythene bag for 10 minutes. Skin and cut into small chunks. Add to the cod.

Peel and chop the onion. Heat half the oil and gently cook the onion for 8–10 minutes until soft. Stir in the remaining oil with the tomato purée, lemon juice and seasoning to taste. Stir into the peppers and cod. Arrange spoonfuls of cod on a plate, garnish with parsley and serve with toast.

Catalan Cod Salad

Serves 4

450 g/1 lb salt cod
1 Spanish onion
1 red pepper
3 ripe tomatoes
salad leaves (optional)
12–16 pitted black olives
1 tsp sweet paprika
2–3 tbsp Spanish extra virgin
olive oil

Prepare and cook the salt cod as described on page 124. When cool, cut the cod into bite-size pieces, place on a plate, cover and leave in the refrigerator while preparing the other ingredients.

Cut the onion in half and thinly slice. Separate the onion slices and reserve.

Preheat the grill and line the grill rack with kitchen foil. Cut the pepper into quarters and discard the seeds. Place skin-side up on the foil-lined grill rack and cook for 8–10 minutes until the skins have blackened. Turn the peppers round to ensure all the skin is blackened. Remove and place in a polythene bag and leave for 10 minutes, then skin. Cut the pepper into small chunks and reserve.

Wash and cut the tomatoes into small chunks, discarding the seeds if preferred. Arrange the salad leaves (if required) in the base of a serving dish. Arrange all the prepared salad ingredients, including the cod and black olives. Sprinkle with the sweet paprika and drizzle over the oil. Cover lightly and keep in the refrigerator. Remove from the refrigerator 15 minutes before serving, to allow to come to room temperature, then serve.

Smoked Mackerel Potato Salad

Serves 4

¹/₂ tsp dry mustard powder
1 large egg yolk
salt and freshly ground
black pepper
150 ml/¹/₄ pint sunflower oil
1–2 tbsp lemon juice
450 g/1 lb baby new potatoes
25 g/1 oz butter
350 g/12 oz smoked mackerel fillets
4 celery stalks, trimmed and
finely chopped
3 tbsp creamed horseradish
150 ml/¹/₄ pint crème fraîche
1 little gem, rinsed and roughly torn
8 cherry tomatoes, halved

Place the mustard powder and egg yolk in a small bowl with salt and pepper and whisk until blended. Add the oil, drop by drop, into the egg mixture, whisking continuously. When the mayonnaise is thick, add the lemon juice, drop by drop, until a smooth, glossy consistency is formed. Reserve.

Cook the potatoes in boiling salted water until tender, then drain. Cool slightly, then cut into halves or quarters, depending on size. Return to the saucepan and toss in the butter.

Remove the skin from the mackerel fillets and flake into pieces. Add to the potatoes in the saucepan, together with the celery.

Blend 4 tablespoons of the mayonnaise with the horseradish and crème fraîche. Season to taste with salt and pepper, then add to the potato and mackerel mixture and stir lightly.

Arrange the lettuce and tomatoes on four serving plates. Pile the smoked mackerel mixture on top of the lettuce, grind over a little pepper and serve with the remaining mayonnaise.

Marinated Mackerel with Tomato Basil Salad

Serves 3

3 mackerel, filleted
3 beef tomatoes, sliced
50 g/2 oz watercress
2 oranges, peeled and segmented
75 g/3 oz mozzarella cheese, sliced
2 tbsp basil leaves, shredded
fresh basil sprigs, to garnish

For the marinade:

juice of 2 lemons
4 tbsp olive oil
4 tbsp basil leaves

For the dressing:

1 tbsp lemon juice
1 tsp Dijon mustard
1 tsp caster sugar
salt and freshly ground black pepper
5 tbsp olive oil

Remove as many of the fine pin bones as possible from the mackerel fillets, lightly rinse and pat dry with absorbent kitchen paper and place in a shallow dish.

Blend the marinade ingredients together and pour over the mackerel fillets. Make sure the marinade has covered the fish completely. Cover and leave in a cool place for at least 8 hours, or preferably overnight. As the fillets marinate, they will lose their translucency and look as if they are cooked.

Place the tomatoes, watercress, oranges and mozzarella cheese in a large bowl and toss.

To make the dressing, whisk the lemon juice with the mustard, sugar, seasoning and olive oil in a bowl. Pour over half the dressing, toss again and then arrange on a serving platter. Remove the mackerel from the marinade, cut into bite-size pieces and sprinkle with the shredded basil. Arrange on top of the salad, drizzle over the remaining dressing, scatter with basil leaves and garnish with a basil sprig. Serve.

Smoked Salmon & Sliced Apple Salad

Serves 4

125 g/4 oz assorted salad leaves
2 eating apples, such as
Granny Smith
3 tbsp lemon juice
175 g/6 oz smoked salmon
2 ripe medium tomatoes
50 g/2 oz black olives, pitted
lemon wedges, to serve

For the dressing:

6 tbsp low-fat Greek yogurt
2 tsp creamed horseradish freshly
ground black pepper

Health Tip

This salad embraces current
thinking in connection to weight
loss – to eat fewer carbohydrates,
a minimal amount of fat and
plenty of protein and vegetables.

Rinse the salad leaves and shake off any excess water, then place on a serving platter or on four individual plates.

Peel the apples if preferred, or rinse lightly, then cut into quarters and discard the cores. Cut into slices and brush with the lemon juice. Reserve both the apples and the lemon juice.

Divide the smoked salmon into pieces and reserve. Rinse the tomatoes and cut into small pieces, then reserve.

To make the dressing, place all the salad dressing ingredients, including the reserved lemon juice, in a screw-top jar, cover with the lid and shake until well blended.

Arrange the prepared ingredients, including the olives, on the platter or plates, then either drizzle the dressing over or hand round separately. Serve with lemon wedges.

Tabbouleh Salad with Quinoa, Salmon & Tomatoes

Serves 4

175 g/6 oz quinoa
350 ml/12 fl oz boiling fish or
vegetable stock, or boiling water
1 medium onion
$^1/_2$ small cucumber
8 ripe baby plum tomatoes
350 g/12 oz canned salmon
2 tbsp extra virgin olive oil
salt and freshly ground
black pepper
$^1/_2$–1 tsp crushed chillies (optional)
2 tbsp freshly chopped parsley,
plus parsley sprigs, to garnish

Place the quinoa in a medium saucepan, cover with the stock or water and bring back to the boil. Cover with the lid, reduce the heat to a simmer and cook for 20–25 minutes until the stock is absorbed and the quinoa is tender. Remove from the heat and fluff up with a fork. Place in a large bowl.

Peel the onion and finely chop, then add to the bowl.

Peel the cucumber and remove the seeds if preferred. Chop or slice the cucumber, then add to the bowl. Rinse the tomatoes, cut in half and add to the bowl.

Drain the salmon and flake, then add to the bowl together with the extra virgin olive oil, seasoning, crushed chillies, if using, and chopped parsley. Stir lightly, then spoon into a serving bowl, garnish with parsley sprigs and serve.

Poached Egg Salad with Smoked Salmon

Serves 4

For the pesto sauce:

50 g/2 oz pine nuts, toasted
(*see* page 36)
2 garlic cloves
50 g/2 oz fresh basil sprigs
150 ml/¼ pint olive oil
50 g/2 oz Parmesan cheese,
freshly grated
crusty bread, to serve

For the salad:

125 g/4 oz assorted salad leaves
125 g/4 oz red or yellow cherry
tomatoes, rinsed
350 g/12 oz smoked salmon slices
4 medium eggs

First, make the pesto sauce. Place the pine nuts and garlic into a food processor and whizz until roughly chopped. Add the basil leaves and stalks and blend again. With the motor running, gradually blend in the olive oil until the sauce is of a pourable consistency. Add the cheese, whizz a little, then scrape into a bowl and reserve.

For the salad, rinse the salad leaves and arrange on a serving plate or four individual plates together with the cherry tomatoes. Arrange the smoked salmon on top.

Bring a frying pan half-filled with water to the boil. When the water is boiling, reduce to a simmer. Carefully crack the eggs into the water and cook for 4 minutes, or until cooked to personal preference. It is easier to cook the eggs if metal rings or cutters are used to contain the egg.

Place the poached eggs on top of the salad. Pour over a little pesto sauce and serve the remainder separately. Serve the salad with crusty bread while the eggs are warm .

Prawn Salad with Toasted Rice

Serves 4

For the dressing:
50 ml/2 fl oz rice vinegar
1 red chilli, deseeded and
thinly sliced
7.5 cm/3 in piece lemongrass
stalk, bruised
juice of 1 lime
2 tbsp Thai fish sauce
1 tsp sugar, or to taste

For the salad:
350 g/12 oz large raw prawns, peeled,
with tails attached, heads removed
salt and freshly ground black pepper
cayenne pepper
1 tbsp long-grain white rice
2 tbsp sunflower oil
1 large head Chinese leaves or
cos lettuce, shredded
1/2 small cucumber, peeled,
deseeded and thinly sliced
1 small bunch chives, cut into
2.5 cm/1 in pieces
small bunch mint leaves

Place all the ingredients for the dressing in a small bowl and leave to stand to let the flavours blend together.

Using a sharp knife, split each prawn lengthways in half, leaving the tail attached to one half. Remove any black veins and pat the prawns dry with absorbent kitchen paper. Sprinkle the prawns with a little salt and cayenne pepper and then reserve.

Heat a wok over a high heat. Add the rice and stir-fry until browned and fragrant. Turn into a mortar and cool. Crush gently with a pestle until coarse crumbs form. Wipe the wok clean.

Reheat the wok, add the oil and, when hot, add the prawns and stir-fry for 2 minutes, or until pink. Transfer to a plate and season to taste with salt and pepper.

Place the Chinese leaves or lettuce into a salad bowl with the cucumber, chives and mint leaves and toss lightly together.

Remove the lemongrass stalk and some of the chilli from the dressing and pour all but 2 tablespoons over the salad and toss until lightly coated. Add the prawns and drizzle with the remaining dressing, then sprinkle with the toasted rice and serve.

Prawn, Avocado Mango Salad

Serves 4

1 large or 2 small ripe mangoes
125 g/4 oz assorted salad leaves
2 celery stalks
125 g/4 oz cherry tomatoes
2 large or 4 small ripe avocados
1 tbsp lemon or orange juice
350 g/12 oz large raw prawns, heads
removed and thawed if frozen
1 tbsp sunflower oil
1–2 tsp reduced-salt soy sauce
freshly ground black pepper

Peel the mangoes and cut away from the stones, then cut the flesh into thin slices and reserve.

Lightly rinse the salad leaves and shake off any excess water. Arrange on four individual plates.

Using a small, sharp knife, trim the celery, then remove any tough strands by making a small slit at the top of each stalk on the outside and pulling down. Repeat three or four times, then slice and scatter over the salad leaves.

Rinse the tomatoes, cut in half and add to the salad. Cut the avocados in half and remove and discard the stones. Peel, then cut into thin slices, then brush with the citrus juice and reserve.

Rinse the prawns and pat dry with absorbent kitchen paper. Heat a wok and add the oil. Heat for 1 minute, then swirl the wok until the sides of the wok are lightly coated in the hot oil. Add the prawns and soy sauce and stir-fry for 3–5 minutes until the prawns have turned pink and are cooked. Drain on absorbent kitchen paper.

Arrange all the reserved ingredients on the plates together with the cooked prawns, add black pepper to taste, then serve.

Thai Prawn Rice Noodle Salad

Serves 4

75 g/3 oz rice vermicelli
175 g/6 oz mangetout, cut in half
crossways
$^1/_2$ cucumber, peeled, deseeded
and diced
2–3 spring onions, trimmed and
thinly sliced diagonally
16–20 large cooked tiger prawns,
peeled, with tails left on
2 tbsp chopped unsalted peanuts
or cashews
lime wedges, to serve
fresh mint sprigs, to garnish

For the dressing:

4 tbsp freshly squeezed lime juice
3 tbsp Thai fish sauce
1 tbsp sugar
2.5 cm/1 in piece fresh root
ginger, peeled and finely chopped
1 red chilli, deseeded and thinly sliced
3–4 tbsp freshly chopped coriander or mint

Place the vermicelli in a bowl and pour over hot water to cover. Leave to stand for 5 minutes, or until softened. Drain, rinse, then drain again and reserve.

Meanwhile, mix all the dressing ingredients in a large bowl until well blended and the sugar has dissolved. Reserve.

Bring a medium saucepan of water to the boil. Add the mangetout, return to the boil and cook for 30–50 seconds. Drain, refresh under cold running water, drain again and reserve.

Stir the cucumber, spring onions and all but four of the prawns into the dressing until lightly coated. Add the mangetout and noodles and toss until all the ingredients are evenly mixed.

Spoon the noodle salad onto warmed individual plates. Sprinkle with peanuts or cashews and garnish each dish with a reserved prawn, a lime wedge and a sprig of mint.

Mussel Tuna Salad

Serves 4

450 g/1 lb fresh mussels
2 shallots, peeled and sliced
1–2 garlic cloves, peeled
small piece celery, trimmed
and chopped
150 ml/¹/₄ pint dry white wine
150 ml/¹/₄ pint water
300 g/11 oz fresh tuna steak
2 tsp olive oil
125 g/4 oz assorted salad leaves
25 g/1 oz sun-dried tomatoes
in oil, drained
4 ripe medium tomatoes
1 small orange pepper
125 g/4 oz feta cheese, drained
25 g/1 oz black olives, pitted
1 tbsp extra virgin olive oil

Scrub the mussels, discarding any beards and barnacles on the shells. Discard any mussels that are open. Place the shallots and garlic with the celery into a large saucepan and add the wine. Bring to the boil and boil for 2 minutes. Add the water and return to the boil before adding the mussels. Cover with a lid and cook for 4–5 minutes until the mussels have opened. Leave until cool, then remove the mussels from the shells. Discard any that are closed. Reserve.

Heat a nonstick frying pan and lightly brush the tuna on both sides with a little olive oil. Place the tuna in the pan and cook for 8–10 minutes until just cooked. Remove, allow to cool, then flake the flesh into pieces and reserve.

Lightly rinse the salad leaves and shake dry. Arrange on a serving platter or four individual dishes. Cut the sun-dried tomatoes into strips. Chop the tomatoes. Cut the pepper into quarters and discard the seeds and membrane, then slice thinly. Cut the feta cheese into cubes.

Arrange all the ingredients, including the mussels, tuna and olives, on the serving platter or on the plates, then drizzle with the extra virgin olive oil and serve.

Seafood Noodle Salad

Serves 4

8 baby squid, cleaned
2 tbsp mirin
2 tbsp rice vinegar
4 tbsp sunflower oil
1 red chilli, deseeded and
finely chopped
2 garlic cloves, peeled and crushed
6 spring onions, trimmed
and finely sliced
1 red pepper, deseeded and
finely sliced
1 tbsp turmeric
2 tsp ground coriander
8 raw tiger prawns, peeled
175 g/6 oz medium egg noodles
175 g/6 oz fresh white crab meat
50 g/2 oz beansprouts
salt and freshly ground
black pepper

Remove the tentacles from the squid and reserve. Slit the squid bodies open down one side and open out flat.

Using a small, sharp knife, score the flesh diagonally, first in one direction, then the other, to make diamond shapes. Place in a bowl with the squid tentacles, mirin, rice vinegar, half the oil and the chilli and leave to marinate in the refrigerator for 1 hour.

Heat a wok until very hot. Add the remaining oil and, when hot, add the garlic, half the spring onions and the red pepper. Stir-fry for 1 minute, then add the turmeric and coriander. Cook for a further 30 seconds before adding the cleaned squid and its marinade and the prawns. Bring to the boil and simmer for 2–3 minutes until the squid and prawns are tender. Remove from the heat and leave to cool.

Cook the noodles for 3–4 minutes until tender, or according to packet instructions. Drain well and put in a large serving bowl along with the white crab meat and the cooled squid and prawn mixture. Stir together and leave until cold. Just before serving, add the beansprouts and remaining spring onions with seasoning to taste, then serve.

Tuna Bean Salad

Serves 4

350 g/12 oz fresh tuna
1–2 tsp olive oil
200 g/7 oz canned beans, such as
haricot or cannellini beans
1 red onion, peeled and sliced
1/2 small cucumber, peeled and
deseeded if preferred
4 medium tomatoes, cut into quarters
50 g/2 oz assorted salad leaves

For the dressing:

1 tbsp extra virgin olive oil
1 tsp sweet chilli sauce, or to taste
2 tbsp orange juice
1/4–1/2 tsp harissa flakes, to taste

Heat a nonstick frying pan and lightly brush the tuna on both sides with the olive oil. Place the tuna in the pan and cook for 8–10 minutes until just cooked. Remove, allow to cool, then flake the flesh into pieces and reserve.

Rinse the beans and place in a bowl together with the red onion slices, cucumber and tomatoes. Divide the salad leaves between four individual serving bowls and put the tuna on top.

Place all the dressing ingredients in a screw-top jar, cover with the lid and shake well. Pour the dressing over the salad and serve.

Ensaladilla

Serves 4

3 large potatoes, peeled
1 large carrot, peeled
125 g/4 oz French beans, trimmed
75 g/3 oz peas
2 bottled artichoke hearts
50 g/2 oz cornichons
2–3 tbsp capers, rinsed
1 red pepper, deseeded
175 g/6 oz canned tuna, drained

For the mayonnaise:

2 medium egg yolks
1 tsp mustard, such as Dijon
150 ml/¼ pint Spanish olive oil
2 tbsp lemon juice
sea salt and freshly ground
black pepper
2 garlic cloves, peeled
and crushed

Cut the potatoes, carrot and beans into small chunks, ensuring they are all similar in size, then cook together with the peas in boiling water until tender. Drain and place in a bowl.

Cut the artichokes and cornichons into small pieces and thoroughly rinse the capers; add to the bowl of vegetables. Cut the pepper into similar size pieces and add to the other vegetables and stir well. Flake the tuna into small pieces and add to the vegetables. Cover and reserve.

Place the egg yolks into a bowl together with the mustard and whisk well. While continuing to whisk, slowly pour in the oil, whisking continuously, adding a little lemon juice as the mayonnaise becomes thick.

When all the oil has been added, add seasoning to taste and the crushed garlic. Continue to add the lemon juice until a smooth, spreadable consistency is achieved.

Add the mayonnaise to the vegetables, stir lightly together and spoon into a serving dish. Cover and leave in a cool place until required.

Fresh Tuna Salad

Serves 4

225 g/8 oz mixed salad leaves
225 g/8 oz baby cherry tomatoes,
halved lengthways
125 g/4 oz rocket leaves, washed
2 tbsp groundnut oil
550 g/1^1/$_5$ lb boned tuna steaks,
each cut into 4 small pieces
50 g/2 oz piece fresh Parmesan
cheese

For the dressing:

8 tbsp olive oil
grated zest and juice of
2 small lemons
1 tbsp wholegrain mustard
salt and freshly ground
black pepper

Wash the salad leaves and place in a large salad bowl with the cherry tomatoes and rocket and reserve.

Heat a wok, then add the oil and heat until almost smoking. Add the tuna, skin-side down, and cook for 4–6 minutes, turning once during cooking until cooked and the flesh flakes easily. Remove from the heat and leave to stand in the juices for 2 minutes before removing.

Meanwhile, make the dressing. Place the olive oil, lemon zest and juices and mustard in a small bowl or screw-top jar and whisk or shake well until well blended. Season to taste with salt and pepper.

Transfer the tuna to a clean chopping board and flake, then add it to the salad and toss lightly.

Using a swivel-blade vegetable peeler, peel the piece of Parmesan cheese into shavings. Divide the salad between four large serving plates, drizzle the dressing over the salad, then scatter with the Parmesan shavings.

Seafood Salad

Serves 4

450 g/1 lb fresh mussels
225 g/8 oz salt cod
225 g/8 oz large cooked prawns
350 g/12 oz crabsticks
1 tbsp Spanish olive oil
125 g/4 oz courgettes, trimmed
and sliced
1 red pepper
125 g/4 oz black olives, pitted
sea salt and freshly ground
black pepper
2 tbsp Spanish extra virgin olive oil
1 tbsp white vinegar
fresh flat-leaf parsley, to garnish

Prepare and cook the mussels as described on page 144, remembering to discard any that are open before cooking and any that are closed after cooking. Prepare, soak and cook the cod as described on page 124.

Place the cooked mussels in a cool place and cover lightly. Discard any skin and bones from the cod, cut into small pieces and reserve.

Peel the prawns and cut the crabsticks into small lengths.

Heat the oil in a frying pan and cook the courgette slices gently for 3–4 minutes until softened, then drain and reserve. Discard the seeds from the pepper and cut into small chunks.

Arrange the seafood in a serving dish with the other ingredients, including the olives. Add seasoning to taste. Blend the extra virgin olive oil and vinegar together, then drizzle over the salad. Garnish with parsley and serve.

Ensaladilla-stuffed Eggs

Serves 4

8 medium eggs
3 tbsp ensaladilla (*see* page 150)
sea salt and freshly ground
black pepper
shredded lettuce, to serve
16 olives stuffed with pimento, cut
in half (optional)
1 red pepper, skinned, or
16 canned anchovy fillets (optional)

Place the eggs into a saucepan and cover with cold water. Bring to the boil and boil gently for 10 minutes. Remove from the hob and plunge into cold water.

Shell the eggs, cut in half, remove the cooked yolk and place in a bowl. Mash with a fork until smooth. Slowly add the ensaladilla and stir into the mashed egg yolk. Add seasoning to taste and reserve.

Carefully fill the hollows in the halved egg whites with the ensaladilla mixture, forking the top to form a neat finish. Arrange some shredded lettuce in the base of the serving dish.

Place the stuffed eggs on top of the lettuce and arrange a halved olive and pepper strip or a canned anchovy on top. Serve.

Broccoli Salad with Sun-dried Tomatoes and Anchovies

Serves 4

350 g/12 oz broccoli florets
$1/4$ tsp sea salt
50 g/2 oz sun-dried tomatoes in oil,
or use olive oil
175 g/6 oz feta cheese
2 tbsp pine nuts
2 x 50 g/2 oz cans anchovy fillets
freshly ground black pepper
crushed chillies, to garnish

Health Tip

All green vegetables play an important part in the diet, as they contain a good proportion of the necessary vitamins and minerals that should be eaten daily. When preparing green vegetables, don't leave them in water to soak, as this will destroy most of the vitamins and minerals, as they will leach out into the water. Always add vegetables to boiling water to preserve their healthy qualities.

Trim the broccoli florets and cut into small pieces. Bring a pan of water to the boil, then add the salt and broccoli. Reduce the heat to a simmer and cover with the lid. Cook for 6–8 minutes until tender but still retain a bite. Drain and plunge into cold water, then, when cool, drain again and place in a bowl.

Cut the sun-dried tomatoes into pieces and drain off 1 tablespoon of their oil, or use olive oil, and reserve.

Cut the feta cheese into cubes and add to the broccoli. Stir and spoon into four individual bowls or one large serving bowl and add the pine nuts.

Drain the oil off the anchovies and blend with the sun-dried tomato oil or olive oil. Pour over the salad. Arrange the anchovy fillets over the salad, season with black pepper to taste and serve garnished with crushed chillies.

Mixed Salad with Anchovy Dressing Ciabatta Croutons

Serves 4

1 small head endive
1 small head chicory
1 fennel bulb
400 g can artichokes, drained and rinsed
1/2 cucumber
125 g/4 oz cherry tomatoes
75 g/3 oz black olives

For the anchovy dressing:

50 g can anchovy fillets
1 tsp Dijon mustard
1 small garlic clove, peeled and crushed
4 tbsp olive oil
1 tbsp lemon juice
freshly ground black pepper

For the ciabatta croutons:

2 thick slices ciabatta bread
2 tbsp olive oil

Divide the endive and chicory into leaves and reserve some of the larger ones. Arrange the smaller leaves in a wide salad bowl.

Cut the fennel bulb in half from the stalk to the root end, then cut across in fine slices. Quarter the artichokes, then quarter and slice the cucumber and halve the tomatoes. Add to the salad bowl with the olives.

To make the dressing, drain the anchovies and put in a blender with the mustard, garlic, olive oil, lemon juice, 2 tablespoons hot water and black pepper. Whizz together until smooth and thickened.

To make the croutons, cut the bread into 1 cm/1/2 inch cubes. Heat the oil in a frying pan, add the bread cubes and fry for 3 minutes, turning frequently, until golden. Remove and drain on absorbent kitchen paper.

Drizzle half the anchovy dressing over the prepared salad and toss to coat. Arrange the reserved endive and chicory leaves around the edge, then drizzle over the remaining dressing. Scatter over the croutons and serve immediately.

Vegetarian

Suited to all kinds of vegetable combinations, salads are the vegetarian's best friend! The recipes in this chapter take inspiration from around the world to bring you the very best in vegetarian salads. For the taste of sunshine in a dish try the Chargrilled Mediterranean Vegetable Salad, or for a Middle Eastern feast the Falafel Salad with Houmous & Olives is the answer.

Winter Coleslaw

Serves 4

175 g/6 oz white cabbage
1 medium red onion, peeled
175 g/6 oz carrot, peeled
175 g/6 oz celeriac, peeled
2 celery stalks, trimmed
75 g/3 oz golden sultanas

For the yogurt & herb dressing:

150 ml/¹/₄ pint low-fat
natural yogurt
1 garlic clove, peeled
and crushed
1 tbsp lemon juice
1 tsp clear honey
1 tbsp freshly snipped chives

Remove the hard core from the cabbage with a small knife and shred finely.

Slice the onion finely and coarsely grate the carrot.

Place the raw vegetables in a large bowl and mix together.

Cut the celeriac into thin strips and simmer in boiling water for about 2 minutes.

Drain the celeriac and rinse thoroughly with cold water.

Chop the celery and add to the bowl with the celeriac and sultanas and mix well.

Make the yogurt and herb dressing by briskly whisking the yogurt, garlic, lemon juice, honey and chives together.

Pour the dressing over the top of the coleslaw. Stir the vegetables thoroughly to coat evenly and serve.

Sicilian Baked Aubergine

Serves 4

1 large aubergine, trimmed
4 large ripe tomatoes
2 celery stalks, trimmed
1 tsp sunflower oil
2 shallots, peeled and
finely chopped
1^1/$_2$ tsp tomato purée
25 g/1 oz pitted green olives
25 g/1 oz pitted black olives
salt and freshly ground
black pepper
1 tbsp white wine vinegar
2 tsp caster sugar
1 tbsp freshly chopped basil,
to garnish
mixed salad leaves, to serve

Preheat the oven to 200°C/400°F/Gas Mark 6. Cut the aubergine into small cubes and place on an oiled baking tray.

Cover the tray with foil and bake in the preheated oven for 15–20 minutes until soft. Reserve, to allow the aubergine to cool.

Cut a cross in the top of each tomato skin, then place with the celery in a large bowl and cover with boiling water.

Remove the tomatoes from the bowl when their skins begin to peel away. Remove the skins, then deseed and chop the flesh into small pieces.

Remove the celery from the bowl of water, chop finely and reserve.

Pour the vegetable oil into a nonstick saucepan, add the chopped shallots and fry gently for 2–3 minutes until soft. Add the celery, tomatoes, tomato purée and olives. Season to taste with salt and pepper.

Simmer gently for 3–4 minutes. Add the vinegar, sugar and cooled aubergine to the pan and heat gently for 2–3 minutes until all the ingredients are well blended. Reserve to allow the aubergine mixture to cool. When cool, garnish with the chopped basil and serve cold with salad leaves.

Aubergine, Tomato Feta Salad

Serves 4

1 small aubergine
salt and freshly ground
black pepper
2–3 tbsp basil-flavoured olive oil
4 medium tomatoes
175 g/6 oz feta cheese
basil leaves, to garnish

Rinse the aubergine and discard the stalk end, then slice thinly. Layer the slices in a colander and sprinkle with a little salt. Leave for 30 minutes to allow the bitter juices to run out. Rinse and pat dry with absorbent kitchen paper.

Line the grill rack with kitchen foil and preheat the grill to medium. Place the aubergine slices in a single layer on the lined rack and brush with a little basil-flavoured oil. Grill for 3–4 minutes until becoming tender, then turn the slices over and brush again with a little oil. Grill for a further 2–3 minutes until the aubergine is cooked. Remove and drain on absorbent kitchen paper. Repeat until all the aubergine slices are cooked.

Rinse the tomatoes, slice to the same thickness as the aubergine and place on a plate. Sprinkle with a tiny amount of salt and black pepper.

Drain the feta cheese and slice to the same thickness as the aubergine and tomatoes. Arrange the aubergine, tomatoes and cheese in a serving dish and pour over any remaining oil. Season to taste, garnish with the basil leaves and serve.

Indonesian Salad with Peanut Dressing

Serves 4

225 g/8 oz new potatoes, scrubbed
1 large carrot, peeled and cut into matchsticks
125 g/4 oz French beans, trimmed
225 g/8 oz tiny cauliflower florets
125 g/4 oz cucumber, cut into matchsticks
75 g/3 oz beansprouts
3 medium eggs, hard-boiled and quartered

For the peanut dressing:

2 tbsp sesame oil
1 garlic clove, peeled and crushed
1 red chilli, deseeded and finely chopped
150 g/5 oz crunchy peanut butter
6 tbsp vegetable stock, heated
2 tsp soft light brown sugar
2 tsp dark soy sauce
1 tbsp lime juice

Cook the potatoes in a saucepan of boiling salted water for 15–20 minutes until tender. Remove with a slotted spoon and slice thickly into a large bowl. Keep the saucepan of water boiling.

Add the carrot, French beans and cauliflower to the water, return to the boil and cook for 2 minutes, or until just tender. Drain and refresh under cold running water, then drain well. Add to the potatoes with the cucumber and beansprouts.

To make the dressing, gently heat the sesame oil in a small saucepan. Add the garlic and chilli and cook for a few seconds, then remove from the heat. Stir in the peanut butter.

Stir in the stock, a little at a time. Add the remaining ingredients and mix together to make a thick, creamy dressing.

Divide the vegetables between four plates and arrange the eggs on top. Drizzle the dressing over the salad and serve immediately.

Mediterranean Rice Salad

Serves 4

250 g/9 oz Camargue red rice
2 sun-dried tomatoes,
finely chopped
2 garlic cloves, peeled and
finely chopped
4 tbsp oil from a jar of sun-dried
tomatoes
2 tsp balsamic vinegar
2 tsp red wine vinegar
salt and freshly ground black pepper
1 red onion, peeled and thinly sliced
1 yellow pepper, quartered
and deseeded
1 red pepper, quartered
and deseeded
1/2 cucumber, peeled and diced
6 ripe plum tomatoes, cut
into wedges
1 fennel bulb, halved and
thinly sliced
fresh basil leaves, to garnish

Cook the rice in a saucepan of lightly salted boiling water for 35–40 minutes until tender. Drain well and reserve.

Whisk the sun-dried tomatoes, garlic, oil and vinegars together in a small bowl or jug. Season to taste with salt and pepper. Put the red onion in a large bowl, pour over the dressing and leave to allow the flavours to develop.

Put the peppers skin-side up on a grill rack and cook under the preheated hot grill for 5–6 minutes until charred. Remove and place in a plastic bag. When cool enough to handle, peel off the skins and slice the peppers.

Add the peppers, cucumber, tomatoes, fennel and rice to the onions. Mix gently together to coat in the dressing. Cover and chill in the refrigerator for 30 minutes to allow the flavours to mingle.

Remove the salad from the refrigerator and leave to stand at room temperature for 20 minutes. Garnish with fresh basil leaves and serve.

Falafel Salad with Houmous Olives

Serves 4

For the falafels:

225 g/8 oz dried chickpeas, soaked
overnight in cold water, or use canned
11 tbsp tahini paste
1 garlic clove, peeled and crushed
sea salt and freshly ground black pepper
1 tsp ground turmeric
$^{1}/_{2}$–1 tsp ground cumin
1 tsp ground coriander
$^{1}/_{4}$ tsp cayenne pepper, or to taste
2 tbsp freshly chopped mint
2 tbsp freshly chopped coriander
1 tbsp plain white flour
2 tbsp vegetable oil
125 g/4 oz assorted salad leaves
50 g/2 oz green olives

For the houmous:

400 g/14 oz can chickpeas
2–3 tbsp lemon juice
1 garlic clove, peeled
4 tbsp tahini paste
salt and freshly ground black pepper

Drain the chickpeas and, if using dried chickpeas, place in a saucepan and completely cover with water. Bring to the boil and remove any scum that rises to the surface. Reduce the heat and simmer for 40 minutes, or until tender, then drain.

Place the chickpeas in a food processor, add the tahini paste and garlic and whizz until the chickpeas are roughly chopped. Add the seasoning and the spices and whizz until the mixture comes together. Scrape into a bowl, cover lightly and leave for 30 minutes before shaping into small patties.

Meanwhile, make the houmous by placing all the ingredients, except the lemon juice, in a food processor and whizzing until smooth. Add enough lemon juice to make a dipping consistency.

When ready to serve, dust the falafel patties in the flour. Heat a little oil in a frying pan and fry over a medium heat for 4–6 minutes until they are heated through and crisp. Drain on absorbent kitchen paper.

Lightly rinse the salad leaves and arrange in a serving dish. Place the falafels on top together with the olives and serve with the houmous.

Pasta Pepper Salad

Serves 4

4 tbsp olive oil
1 each red, orange and yellow
pepper, deseeded and cut
into chunks
1 large courgette, trimmed and cut
into chunks
1 medium aubergine, trimmed
and diced
275 g/10 oz fusilli
4 plum tomatoes, quartered
1 bunch fresh basil leaves,
roughly chopped
2 tbsp pesto
2 garlic cloves, peeled and
roughly chopped
1 tbsp lemon juice
225 g/8 oz skinless, boneless roasted
chicken breast (optional)
salt and freshly ground black pepper
125 g/4 oz feta cheese, crumbled
crusty bread, to serve

Preheat the oven to 200°C/400°F/Gas Mark 6. Spoon the olive oil into a roasting tin and heat in the oven for 2 minutes, or until almost smoking. Remove from the oven, add the peppers, courgette and aubergine and stir until coated. Bake for 30 minutes, or until charred, stirring occasionally.

Bring a large pan of lightly salted water to a rolling boil. Add the pasta and cook according to the packet instructions, or until *al dente*. Drain and refresh under cold running water. Drain thoroughly, place in a large salad bowl and reserve.

Remove the cooked vegetables from the oven and allow to cool. Add to the cooled pasta together with the quartered tomatoes, chopped basil leaves, pesto, garlic and lemon juice. Toss lightly to mix.

If using chicken, shred it roughly into small pieces and stir into the pasta and vegetable mixture. Season to taste with salt and pepper, then sprinkle the crumbled feta cheese over the pasta and stir gently. Cover the dish and leave to marinate for 30 minutes, stirring occasionally. Serve the salad with fresh crusty bread.

Venetian Herb Orzo

Serves 4–6

200 g/7 oz baby spinach leaves
150 g/5 oz rocket leaves
50 g/2 oz flat-leaf parsley
few fresh mint leaves
6 spring onions, trimmed
3 tbsp extra virgin olive oil, plus
more if required
450 g/1 lb orzo
salt and freshly ground
black pepper

Rinse the spinach leaves in several changes of cold water and reserve. Finely chop the rocket leaves with the parsley and mint. Thinly slice the green of the spring onions.

Bring a large saucepan of water to the boil, add the spinach leaves, herbs and spring onions and cook for about 10 seconds. Remove and rinse under cold running water. Drain well and, using your hands, squeeze out all the excess moisture.

Place the spinach, herbs and spring onions in a food processor. Blend for 1 minute, then, with the motor running, gradually pour in the olive oil until the sauce is well blended.

Meanwhile, bring a large pan of lightly salted water to a rolling boil. Add the pasta and cook according to the packet instructions, or until *al dente*. Drain thoroughly and place in a large, warmed bowl.

Add the spinach sauce to the orzo and stir lightly until the orzo is well coated. Stir in an extra tablespoon of olive oil if the mixture seems too thick. Season well with salt and pepper. Serve immediately on warmed plates or allow to cool to room temperature.

Quinoa Roasted Vegetable Salad

Serves 4

1 medium red onion
2–3 garlic cloves
1–2 red peppers
1 small aubergine
1 large courgette
2–3 tbsp olive oil
salt and freshly ground
black pepper
3 medium tomatoes
225 g/8 oz quinoa
1 litre/1³/4 pint boiling vegetable
stock or water
175 g/6 oz canned chickpeas
lemon balm sprigs, to garnish

Preheat the oven to 180°C/350°F/Gas Mark 4, 10 minutes before roasting the vegetables.

Peel and slice the onion, then peel and crush the garlic, Cut the peppers into quarters, discard the seeds and cut into small pieces. Place in a roasting tin. Discard the stalk end from the aubergine and courgette and dice. Place in the roasting tin and pour over the oil. Season, then roast in the oven for 20 minutes, stirring at least twice during cooking.

About 5 minutes before the end of the roasting time, cut the tomatoes into small pieces and add to the roasting tin.

Meanwhile, place the quinoa in a medium saucepan and stir in the boiling stock or water. Place over a low heat and cook for 15–20 minutes until the quinoa is cooked.

When the vegetables are cooked, cool slightly, then stir into the quinoa together with the chickpeas. Spoon into a serving dish, garnish with the lemon balm sprigs and serve.

Cold Sesame Noodles

Serves 4–8

450 g/1 lb buckwheat (soba)
noodles or wholewheat spaghetti
1 tbsp sesame oil
1 tbsp groundnut oil
1 green pepper, deseeded and
thinly sliced
125 g/4 oz daikon (mooli), cut into
julienne strips
125 g/4 oz mangetout or green
beans, trimmed and sliced
2 garlic cloves, peeled and
finely chopped
2 tbsp soy sauce, or to taste
1 tbsp cider vinegar
2 tbsp sweet chilli sauce, or to taste
2 tsp sugar
75 g/3 oz peanut butter
salt
6–8 spring onions, trimmed and
diagonally sliced

To garnish:

toasted sesame seeds
cucumber strips

Bring a large pan of lightly salted water to a rolling boil. Add the noodles or spaghetti and cook according to the packet instructions, or until *al dente*. Drain, rinse and drain again, then toss in the sesame oil and reserve.

Heat the groundnut oil in a wok or large frying pan over a high heat. Add the green pepper, daikon and mangetout or green beans and stir-fry for 1 minute. Stir in the garlic and cook for 30 seconds.

Add the soy sauce to the pan with the vinegar, chilli sauce, sugar, peanut butter and 50 ml/2 fl oz hot water. Simmer, stirring continuously, until the peanut butter is smooth, adding a little more water if necessary and adjusting the seasoning to taste.

Add the spring onions and the reserved noodles or spaghetti to the peanut sauce and cook, stirring, for 2–3 minutes until heated through. Tip the mixture into a large serving bowl and allow to cool to room temperature, stirring occasionally. Garnish with the toasted sesame seeds and cucumber julienne strips before serving.

Tortellini Summer Vegetable Salad

Serves 6

350 g/12 oz mixed green and plain cheese-filled fresh tortellini
150 ml/¼ pint extra virgin olive oil
225 g/8 oz fine green beans, trimmed
175 g/6 oz broccoli florets
1 yellow or red pepper, deseeded and thinly sliced
1 red onion, peeled and sliced
175 g jar marinated artichoke hearts, drained and halved
2 tbsp capers
75 g/3 oz dry-cured, pitted black olives
3 tbsp raspberry or balsamic vinegar
1 tbsp Dijon mustard
1 tsp soft brown sugar
salt and freshly ground black pepper
2 tbsp freshly chopped basil or flat-leaf parsley
2 quartered hard-boiled eggs, to garnish

Bring a large pan of lightly salted water to a rolling boil. Add the tortellini and cook according to the packet instructions, or until *al dente*.

Using a large slotted spoon, transfer the tortellini to a colander to drain. Rinse under cold running water and drain again. Transfer to a large bowl and toss with 2 tablespoons of the olive oil.

Return the pasta water to the boil and drop in the green beans and broccoli florets; blanch them for 2 minutes, or until just beginning to soften. Drain, rinse under cold running water and drain again thoroughly. Add the vegetables to the reserved tortellini.

Add the pepper, onion, artichoke hearts, capers and olives to the bowl; stir lightly.

Whisk together the vinegar, mustard and brown sugar in a bowl and season to taste with salt and pepper. Slowly whisk in the remaining olive oil to form a thick, creamy dressing. Pour over the tortellini and vegetables, add the chopped basil or parsley and stir until lightly coated. Transfer to a shallow serving dish or salad bowl. Garnish with the hard-boiled egg quarters and serve.

Grilled Pear, Asparagus & Blue Cheese Salad

Serves 4

225 g/8 oz fresh asparagus
salt and freshly ground
black pepper
4 ripe pears
2–3 tbsp olive oil, or use a flavoured
oil such as chilli-flavoured oil
125 g/4 oz assorted salad leaves
175 g/6 oz soft, creamy blue
cheese, such as Roquefort
$^1/_2$–1 tsp paprika

Trim the asparagus, discarding the tough, woody part of the stem. Using a vegetable peeler, peel the remaining stem so that the stem is tender, then cut into 10 cm/4 inch pieces.

Bring a shallow pan, such as a frying pan, half-filled with water to the boil and add a little salt. Cook the asparagus for 5–8 minutes until it is just tender. Drain and reserve.

Line the grill rack with kitchen foil and preheat the grill to medium. Rinse the pears and peel if preferred. Cut in half and discard the cores.

Place the cooked asparagus and the pear halves on the lined grill rack and brush with the oil. Grill for 6–8 minutes until lightly charred, turning the asparagus and pears over at least once and brushing with extra oil if necessary during cooking.

Rinse the salad leaves and shake off any excess water. Arrange in a serving dish together with the asparagus.

Cut some of the pears into small pieces and place both halved and pieces of pear on top of the salad leaves. Cut the cheese into various size pieces and dot over the salad. Sprinkle with the paprika and serve.

Oriental Noodle Peanut Salad with Coriander

Serves 4

350 g/12 oz rice vermicelli
1 litre/1³/₄ pints light chicken stock
2 tsp sesame oil
2 tbsp light soy sauce
8 spring onions
3 tbsp groundnut oil
2 hot green chillies, deseeded and thinly sliced
25 g/1 oz roughly chopped coriander
2 tbsp freshly chopped mint
125 g/4 oz cucumber, finely chopped
40 g/1¹/₂ oz beansprouts
40 g/1¹/₂ oz roasted peanuts, roughly chopped

Put the noodles into a large bowl. Bring the stock to the boil and immediately pour over the noodles. Leave to soak for 4 minutes, or according to the packet instructions. Drain well, discarding the stock or saving it for another use. Mix together the sesame oil and soy sauce and pour over the hot noodles. Toss well to coat and leave until cold.

Trim and thinly slice 4 of the spring onions. Heat the oil in a wok over a low heat. Add the spring onions and, as soon as they sizzle, remove from the heat and leave to cool. When cold, toss with the noodles.

On a chopping board, cut the remaining spring onions lengthways four to six times; leave in a bowl of cold water until tassels form. Serve the noodles in individual bowls, each dressed with a little chilli, coriander, mint, cucumber, beansprouts and peanuts. Garnish with the spring onion tassels and serve.

Crispy Noodle Salad

Serves 4

2 tbsp sunflower seeds
2 tbsp pumpkin seeds
50 g/2 oz rice vermicelli or
stir-fry noodles
175 g/6 oz unsalted butter
2 tbsp sesame seeds,
lightly toasted
125 g/4 oz red cabbage, trimmed
and shredded
1 orange pepper, deseeded and
finely chopped
125 g/4 oz button mushrooms,
wiped and quartered
2 spring onions, trimmed and
finely chopped
salt and freshly ground
black pepper
shredded pickled sushi ginger,
to garnish

Preheat the oven to 200°C/400°F/Gas Mark 6, then sprinkle the sunflower and pumpkin seeds on a baking sheet. Toast in the oven, stirring occasionally, for 10–15 minutes until lightly toasted. Remove from the oven and leave to cool.

Crush the rice vermicelli into small pieces (this is easiest in a plastic bag or while the noodles are still in the packet) and reserve. Melt the butter in a small saucepan and leave to cool for a few minutes. Pour the clear, yellow liquid carefully into a bowl, leaving behind the white, milky solids. Discard the milky solids.

Heat the yellow, clarified butter in a wok and fry the crushed noodles in batches until browned, stirring continuously and gently. Remove the fried noodles as they cook, using a slotted spoon, and drain on absorbent kitchen paper. Transfer the noodles to a bowl and add the toasted seeds.

Mix together the red cabbage, orange pepper, button mushrooms and spring onions in a large bowl and season to taste with salt and pepper. Just before serving, add the noodles and seeds to the salad and mix gently. Garnish with a little sushi ginger and serve.

Chargrilled Mediterranean Vegetable Salad

Serves 4

1 small aubergine
salt and freshly ground
black pepper
1 medium onion
2–3 garlic cloves
2 small red peppers
1 large courgette
4 medium tomatoes
2 tbsp olive oil
175 g/6 oz assorted salad leaves
175 g/6 oz feta cheese
50 g/2 oz black olives,
preferably pitted

For the dressing:

1 tbsp olive oil
2 tbsp balsamic vinegar

Rinse the aubergine and discard the stalk end. Slice thinly. Layer the slices in a colander and sprinkle with a little salt. Leave for 30 minutes to allow the bitter juices to run out. Rinse and pat dry with absorbent kitchen paper.

Peel the onion and slice, then peel and crush the garlic. Cut the peppers into quarters, discard the seeds and cut into small pieces.

Trim the courgette and slice thinly, then cut the tomatoes into quarters. Place all the vegetables in a large bowl, pour over the oil and toss until all the vegetables are lightly coated in the oil.

Rinse the salad leaves and shake off any excess water, then arrange in a serving dish and reserve. Drain the feta cheese, cut into dice and reserve.

Heat a large griddle pan and add the vegetables. (You may need to do this in batches or use a large, nonstick frying pan.) Cook for 12–15 minutes, stirring frequently, until the vegetables are lightly charred. Stir the feta cheese into the vegetables, then place on top of the salad leaves with the olives. Mix the olive oil and balsamic vinegar together and drizzle over the top, then serve.

Red Pepper Salad

Serves 4

4 red peppers
150 ml/¹/₄ pint Spanish olive oil
50 g/2 oz capers in brine
3–4 garlic cloves, peeled
salt and freshly ground
black pepper
1 tsp caster sugar
2 tbsp sherry vinegar
1 tbsp freshly snipped
chives (optional)

Preheat the oven to 200°C/400°F/Gas Mark 6, 15 minutes before roasting the peppers.

Rinse the peppers. Either leave the peppers whole or cut into quarters. If leaving whole, carefully cut a circle around the stalk, then pull and remove the seeds. Alternatively, cut into quarters and remove the seeds.

Place in a roasting tin, pour over 3 tablespoons of the oil, then place in the oven and roast for 15–20 minutes until soft, basting the peppers during roasting. Remove from the oven, reserving the oil.

Drain the capers and rinse thoroughly. Place the peppers and the peeled garlic into a dish and scatter with the capers. Blend the remaining oil with the oil used in cooking, then season to taste with salt and pepper and sprinkle with the sugar and vinegar. Pour over the peppers and leave to marinate for at least 2 hours, longer if time permits, turning the peppers over occasionally.

Serve with the chives, if using, sprinkled over.

Artichokes in Vinaigrette

Serves 4

4 artichokes
2 tbsp Spanish olive oil
2 tbsp lemon juice
sea salt and freshly ground
black pepper
freshly chopped flat-leaf parsley,
to garnish (optional)

For the vinaigrette:

$^1/_2$ tsp mustard powder
1 tsp caster sugar or clear honey
2 tsp sherry or white wine vinegar
6 tbsp Spanish virgin olive oil
2 tbsp lemon juice
1 tbsp freshly chopped parsley

Pull off and discard the bottom leaves of the artichokes if they are damaged, then cut the stalk off each artichoke so that it is level with the bottom leaves. Trim the remaining leaves and cut the tops so that they are level. Thoroughly wash under cold running water.

Stand the prepared artichokes in a deep saucepan or pot with 7.5 cm/3 inches boiling water. Pour in 1 tablespoon of the oil with the lemon juice and seasoning. Cover with the lid and bring to a gentle boil and simmer for 30–40 minutes until a leaf near the centre pulls out easily. When cooked, remove from the pan and stand the artichokes upside down on a rack to drain. Cool, then cut into quarters and place in a dish.

Place all the ingredients for the vinaigrette in a screw-top jar, add seasoning and shake vigorously. Put the artichokes into the vinaigrette in a bowl to marinate, either overnight or until the artichokes have absorbed the flavour of the vinaigrette. Serve garnished with parsley, if using.

Quinoa Salad with Broad Beans & Parmesan

Serves 4

225 g/8 oz red quinoa
1 litre heated vegetable stock
or water
$^{1}/_{2}$–1 tsp ground coriander
$^{1}/_{2}$ tsp ground cumin
salt and freshly ground
black pepper
225 g/8 oz shelled broad beans
1–2 red peppers
50 g/2 oz black olives,
preferably pitted
7.5 cm/3 in piece cucumber
2 tbsp extra virgin olive oil
25 g/1 oz Parmesan or vegetarian
Italian hard cheese,
finely grated
1 lemon, cut into wedges
(optional)

Place the quinoa in a medium saucepan and stir in the heated stock or water. Place over a low heat and cook for 15–20 minutes until the quinoa is cooked. Stir in the spices with seasoning to taste. Reserve.

Half-fill a medium saucepan with water and bring to the boil. Add the shelled broad beans and return to the boil. Reduce the heat to a simmer and cook for 10–12 minutes until tender. Drain and allow to cool. When cool enough to handle, remove the outer casings, then stir the peeled broad beans into the quinoa. Reserve.

Line a grill rack with kitchen foil and preheat the grill to medium. Cut the peppers into quarters and discard the seeds and membranes. Place the peppers on the lined rack and grill for 10 minutes, or until the skins have wrinkled and started to blister. Remove and allow to cool. When cool, cut into small pieces and stir into the quinoa.

Drain the olives if in brine, add to the quinoa and stir lightly. Peel the cucumber if preferred and slice, then add to the quinoa. Drizzle with the olive oil. Just before serving, sprinkle with the grated Parmesan or vegetarian hard cheese and garnish with the lemon wedges, if using.

Catalan Roasted Vegetable Salad

Serves 4–6

2 medium onions
3–4 garlic cloves
1 small aubergine
1 red pepper
1 yellow pepper
4 firm but ripe tomatoes
2 tbsp Spanish olive oil
2 tbsp lemon juice
1 tbsp sherry vinegar
1 tsp Spanish paprika

Preheat the oven to 180°C/350°F/Gas Mark 4, 10 minutes before cooking.

Peel the onions and garlic and leave whole. Trim the stalk from the aubergine, then rinse the aubergine and peppers. Place the onions in a roasting tin and cook for 10 minutes. Reserve one garlic clove and add all the vegetables, including the tomatoes, to the onions in the tin. Drizzle with 1 tablespoon of the oil and continue to cook for a further 20–25 minutes until the vegetables are tender. Turn the vegetables over a couple of times during cooking. Remove from the oven and leave until cool enough to handle.

Cut the onion into small wedges. Chop the garlic if liked, and cut the aubergine into small chunks. Cut the peppers into quarters, discard the seeds, then chop into small pieces. Reserve half the tomatoes and skin them, then cut the remaining tomatoes into pieces. Place all the prepared vegetables in a serving dish.

Place all the remaining ingredients in a food processor together with the reserved tomatoes and blend to form a smooth dressing. Pour over the vegetables and serve.

Pasta Salad with Courgettes, Rosemary & Lemon

Serves 4

350 g/12 oz dried pasta shapes,
such as rigatoni
1¹/₂ tbsp good-quality extra virgin
olive oil
2 garlic cloves, peeled and
finely chopped
4 medium courgettes, thinly sliced
1 tbsp freshly chopped rosemary
1 tbsp freshly chopped parsley
zest and juice of 2 lemons
25 g/1 oz pitted black olives,
roughly chopped
25 g/1 oz pitted green olives,
roughly chopped
salt and freshly ground
black pepper

To garnish:

lemon slices
fresh rosemary sprigs

Bring a large saucepan of salted water to the boil and add the pasta.

Return to the boil and cook until *al dente*, or according to the packet instructions.

Meanwhile, when the pasta is almost done, heat the oil in a large frying pan and add the garlic.

Cook over a medium heat until the garlic is just beginning to brown. Be careful not to overcook the garlic at this stage or it will become bitter.

Add the courgettes, rosemary, parsley and lemon zest and juice. Cook for 3–4 minutes until the courgettes are just tender.

Add the olives to the frying pan and stir well. Season to taste with salt and pepper and remove from the heat.

Drain the pasta well and add to the frying pan. Stir until thoroughly combined. Garnish with lemon and sprigs of fresh rosemary. Allow to cool and serve as a salad.

Caprese Salad

Serves 4

4 large ripe beef tomatoes
4 balls buffalo mozzarella cheese
2–3 tbsp extra virgin olive oil
freshly ground black pepper
about 15 g/^{1}/$_2$ oz basil leaves

Health Tip

There are literally hundreds of varieties of tomatoes, ranging from tiny cherry tomatoes about the size of an olive to very large varieties about the size of a large orange. Tomatoes are very healthy and contain lycopene, which has been linked to bone health. The intake of fresh tomatoes and tomato products has long been shown to be helpful in reducing the bad LDL cholesterol, as well as helping to prevent blood platelets clumping together in the blood to help prevent heart disease and other heart-related diseases.

Lightly rinse the tomatoes and cut into medium slices. Reserve.

Drain the cheese and cut into slices about a similar thickness to the tomatoes.

Arrange the sliced tomatoes and cheese in a serving dish and pour over the olive oil. Season to taste with black pepper.

Lightly crush the basil leaves to help extract the flavour, then scatter the basil over the tomatoes and cheese and serve.

Creamy Puy Lentils

Serves 4

225 g/8 oz Puy lentils
1 tbsp olive oil
1 garlic clove, peeled and
finely chopped
zest and juice of 1 lemon
1 tsp wholegrain mustard
1 tbsp freshly chopped tarragon
3 tbsp half-fat crème fraîche
salt and freshly ground
black pepper
2 small tomatoes, deseeded
and chopped
50 g/2 oz pitted black olives
1 tbsp freshly chopped parsley

To garnish:

fresh tarragon sprigs
lemon wedges

Put the lentils in a saucepan with plenty of cold water and bring to the boil. Boil rapidly for 10 minutes, reduce the heat and simmer gently for a further 20 minutes until just tender. Drain well.

Meanwhile, prepare the dressing. Heat the oil in a frying pan over a medium heat. Add the garlic and cook for about a minute until just beginning to brown. Add the lemon zest and juice.

Add the mustard and cook for a further 30 seconds. Add the tarragon and crème fraîche and season to taste with salt and pepper. Simmer and add the drained lentils, tomatoes and olives. Transfer to a serving dish and sprinkle the chopped parsley on top.

Garnish the lentils with the tarragon sprigs and the lemon wedges and serve immediately.

Fusilli Pasta Salad with Spicy Tomato Salsa

Serves 4

6 large ripe tomatoes
2 tbsp lemon juice
2 tbsp lime juice
grated zest of 1 lime
2 shallots, peeled and
finely chopped
2 garlic cloves, peeled
and finely chopped
1–2 red chillies
1–2 green chillies
450 g/1 lb fresh fusilli pasta
4 tbsp half-fat crème fraîche
2 tbsp freshly chopped basil
oregano sprig, to garnish

Cut a cross in the skin of each tomato, place in a bowl and cover with boiling water. Allow to stand until the skins start to peel away.

Remove the skins from the tomatoes, divide each tomato into four quarters and remove all the seeds. Chop the flesh into small dice and put in a small pan. Add the lemon and lime juice and the grated lime zest and stir well.

Add the chopped shallots and garlic. Remove the seeds carefully from the chillies, chop finely and add to the pan.

Bring to the boil and simmer gently for 5–10 minutes until the salsa has thickened slightly.

Reserve the salsa to allow it to cool and the flavours to develop while the pasta is cooking.

Bring a large pan of water to the boil and add the pasta. Simmer gently for 3–4 minutes until the pasta is just tender.

Drain the pasta and refresh under cold water. Place in a serving dish and top with a large spoonful of salsa and a small spoonful of crème fraîche. Garnish with the basil and oregano and serve.

Pasta with Raw Fennel, Tomato & Red Onions

Serves 6

1 fennel bulb
700 g/1¹/₂ lb tomatoes
1 garlic clove
¹/₄ small red onion
small handful fresh basil
small handful fresh mint
100 ml/3¹/₂ fl oz extra virgin olive oil, plus extra to serve
juice of 1 lemon
salt and freshly ground black pepper
450 g/1 lb penne or pennette
freshly grated Parmesan or vegetarian Italian hard cheese, to serve

Trim the fennel and slice thinly. Stack the slices and cut into sticks, then cut crossways again into fine dice. Deseed the tomatoes and chop them finely. Peel and finely chop or crush the garlic. Peel and finely chop or grate the onion.

Stack the basil leaves, then roll up tightly. Slice crossways into fine shreds. Finely chop the mint.

Place the chopped vegetables and herbs in a medium bowl. Add the olive oil and lemon juice and mix together. Season well with salt and pepper, then leave for 30 minutes to allow the flavours to develop.

Bring a large pan of salted water to a rolling boil. Add the pasta and cook according to the packet instructions, or until *al dente*.

Drain the cooked pasta thoroughly and refresh under cold water. Transfer to a serving dish, pour over the vegetable mixture and toss. Serve with the grated Parmesan or vegetarian hard cheese and extra olive oil to drizzle over.

Pasta Salad with Spicy Red Pepper Sauce

Serves 4

2 red peppers
2 tbsp olive oil
1 onion, peeled and chopped
2 garlic cloves, peeled and crushed
1 red chilli, deseeded and finely chopped
200 g/7 oz can chopped tomatoes
finely grated zest and juice of $1/2$ lemon
salt and freshly ground black pepper
2–3 tbsp vegetable stock (optional)
400 g/14 oz dried pasta, such as tagliatelle, linguine or shells

To garnish:

shaved Parmesan or vegetarian Italian hard cheese,
fresh basil leaves

Preheat the grill. Set the whole peppers on the grill rack about 10 cm/ 4 inches away from the heat, then grill, turning frequently, for 10 minutes until the skins are blackened and blistered.

Put the peppers in a plastic bag and leave until cool enough to handle. Peel off the skin, then halve the peppers and scrape away the seeds. Chop the pepper flesh roughly and put in a food processor or blender.

Heat the olive oil in a large saucepan and gently fry the onion for 5 minutes. Stir in the garlic and chilli and cook for a further 5 minutes, stirring. Add to the food processor and blend until fairly smooth.

Return the mixture to the saucepan with the tomatoes and stir in the lemon zest and juice. Season to taste with salt and pepper. Add 2–3 tablespoons vegetable stock if the sauce is a little thick. Bring to the boil and bubble for 1–2 minutes, then allow to cool.

Meanwhile, bring a large saucepan of lightly salted water to the boil and cook the pasta for 10 minutes, or until *al dente*. Drain thoroughly and refresh under cold water. Add the sauce and toss well to coat.

Tip into a serving dish or onto individual plates. Scatter with shavings of cheese and a few basil leaves before serving.

Warm

Salads

Enjoying great salads doesn't have to be limited to the summer months when the weather is hot; instead, a warm salad can be an excellent way to brighten up a chilly day. Featuring seasonal vegetables and stunning flavour combinations, the warm salads in this chapter will help you satisfy your salad cravings throughout the year. Why not try the Warm Chard Salad with Anchovies & Garlic – perfect for a winter's lunch – or the delicious Hot Duck Pasta Salad, which is both nutritious and satisfying?

Oriental Minced Chicken on Rocket Tomato

Serves 4

2 shallots, peeled
1 garlic clove, peeled
1 carrot, peeled
50 g/2 oz water chestnuts
1 tsp olive oil
350 g/12 oz fresh
chicken mince
1 tsp Chinese five-spice powder
pinch chilli powder
1 tsp soy sauce
1 tbsp fish sauce
8 cherry tomatoes
50 g/2 oz rocket

Finely chop the shallots and garlic. Cut the carrot into matchsticks, thinly slice the water chestnuts and reserve. Heat the oil in a wok or large, heavy-based frying pan and add the chicken. Stir-fry for 3–4 minutes over a moderately high heat, breaking up any large pieces of chicken.

Add the garlic and shallots and cook for 2–3 minutes until softened. Sprinkle over the Chinese five-spice powder and the chilli powder and continue to cook for about 1 minute.

Add the carrot, water chestnuts, soy and fish sauces and 2 tablespoons water. Stir-fry for a further 2 minutes. Remove from the heat and reserve to cool slightly.

Deseed the tomatoes and cut into thin wedges. Toss with the rocket and divide between four serving plates. Spoon the warm chicken mixture over the rocket and tomato wedges and serve immediately to prevent the rocket from wilting.

Wild Rice Bacon Salad with Smoked Chicken

Serves 4

150 g/5 oz wild rice
50 g/2 oz pecan or walnut halves
1 tbsp vegetable oil
4 slices smoked bacon, diced
3–4 shallots, peeled and
finely chopped
75 ml/3 fl oz walnut oil
2–3 tbsp sherry or cider vinegar
2 tbsp freshly chopped dill
salt and freshly ground
black pepper
275 g/10 oz smoked chicken or
duck breast, thinly sliced
dill sprigs, to garnish

Put the wild rice in a medium saucepan with 600 ml/1 pint water and bring to the boil, stirring once or twice. Reduce the heat, cover and simmer gently for 30–50 minutes, depending on the texture you prefer, chewy or tender. Using a fork, gently fluff into a large bowl and leave to cool slightly.

Meanwhile, toast the nuts in a frying pan over a medium heat for 2 minutes, or until they are fragrant and lightly coloured, stirring and tossing frequently. Cool, then chop coarsely and add to the rice.

Heat the oil in the frying pan over a medium heat. Add the bacon and cook, stirring occasionally, for 3–4 minutes until crisp and brown. Remove from the pan and drain on absorbent kitchen paper. Add the shallots to the pan and cook for 4 minutes, or until just softened, stirring occasionally. Stir into the rice and nuts with the drained bacon pieces.

Whisk the walnut oil, vinegar, half the dill and salt and pepper in a small bowl until combined. Pour the dressing over the rice mixture and toss well to combine. Mix the chicken and the remaining chopped dill into the rice, then spoon into bowls and garnish each serving with a dill sprig. Serve slightly warm, or at room temperature.

Warm Chicken & Potato Salad with Peas & Mint

Serves 4–6

450 g/1 lb new potatoes, peeled
or scrubbed and cut into
bite-size pieces
2 tbsp cider vinegar
175 g/6 oz frozen garden
peas, thawed
1 small, ripe avocado
4 cooked chicken breasts,
about 450g/1 lb in weight,
skinned and diced
2 tbsp freshly chopped mint
2 heads little gem lettuce
fresh mint sprigs, to garnish

For the dressing:

2 tbsp raspberry or sherry vinegar
2 tsp Dijon mustard
1 tsp clear honey
50 ml/2 fl oz sunflower oil
50 ml/2 fl oz extra virgin olive oil
salt and freshly ground black pepper

Cook the potatoes in lightly salted boiling water for 15 minutes, or until just tender when pierced with the tip of a sharp knife; do not overcook. Rinse under cold running water to cool slightly, then drain and turn into a large bowl. Sprinkle with the cider vinegar and toss gently.

Run the peas under hot water to ensure that they are thawed, pat dry with absorbent kitchen paper and add to the potatoes.

Cut the avocado in half lengthways and remove the stone. Peel and cut the avocado into cubes and add to the potatoes and peas. Add the chicken and stir together lightly.

To make the dressing, place all the ingredients in a screw-top jar with a little salt and pepper and shake well to mix; add a little more oil if the flavour is too sharp. Pour over the salad and toss gently to coat. Sprinkle in half the mint and stir lightly.

Separate the lettuce leaves and spread onto a large, shallow serving plate. Spoon the salad on top and sprinkle with the remaining mint. Garnish with mint sprigs and serve.

Spicy Chicken Skewers with Mango Tabbouleh

Serves 4

400 g/14 oz chicken breast fillet
200 ml/7 fl oz low-fat natural yogurt
1 garlic clove, peeled and crushed
1 small red chilli, deseeded and
finely chopped
1/2 tsp ground turmeric
finely grated zest and juice
of 1/2 lemon
fresh mint sprigs, to garnish

For the mango tabbouleh:

175 g/6 oz bulgur wheat
1 tsp olive oil
juice of 1/2 lemon
1/2 red onion, finely chopped
1 ripe mango, halved, stoned,
peeled and chopped
1/4 cucumber, finely diced
2 tbsp freshly chopped parsley
2 tbsp freshly shredded mint
salt and freshly ground black pepper

If using wooden skewers, pre-soak them in cold water for at least 30 minutes. (This stops them from burning during grilling.) Cut the chicken into five1 cm/2 x 1/2 inch strips and place in a shallow dish. Mix together the yogurt, garlic, chilli, turmeric, lemon zest and juice. Pour over the chicken and toss to coat. Cover and leave to marinate in the refrigerator for up to 8 hours.

To make the tabbouleh, put the bulgur wheat in a bowl. Pour over enough boiling water to cover. Put a plate over the bowl. Leave to soak for 20 minutes.

Whisk together the oil and lemon juice in a bowl. Add the red onion and leave to marinate for 10 minutes.

Drain the bulgur wheat and squeeze out any excess moisture in a clean tea towel. Add to the red onion with the mango, cucumber and herbs and season to taste with salt and pepper. Toss together.

Thread the chicken strips onto eight wooden or metal skewers. Cook under a hot grill for 8 minutes. Turn and brush with the marinade and grill until the chicken is lightly browned and cooked through. Spoon the tabbouleh onto individual plates. Arrange the chicken skewers on top and garnish with the sprigs of mint. Serve warm or cold.

Hot Duck Pasta Salad

Serves 6

3 skinless and boneless
duck breasts
1 tbsp wholegrain mustard
1 tbsp clear honey
salt and freshly ground black pepper
4 medium eggs
125 g/4 oz French beans, trimmed
450 g/1 lb fusilli
1 large carrot, peeled and cut into
thin batons
125 g/4 oz sweetcorn kernels,
cooked if frozen
75 g/3 oz fresh baby spinach
leaves, shredded

For the dressing:

8 tbsp French dressing
1 tsp horseradish sauce
4 tbsp crème fraîche

Preheat the oven to 200°C/400°F/Gas Mark 6. Place the duck breasts on a baking tray lined with foil. Mix together the wholegrain mustard and honey, season lightly with salt and pepper, then spread over the duck breasts. Roast in the preheated oven for 20–30 minutes until tender. Remove from the oven and keep warm.

Meanwhile, place the eggs in a small saucepan, cover with water and bring to the boil. Simmer for 8 minutes, then drain. Bring a large pan of lightly salted water to a rolling boil. Add the beans and pasta, return to the boil and cook according to the packet instructions, or until *al dente*. Drain the pasta and beans and refresh under cold running water.

Place the pasta and beans in a bowl, add the carrot, sweetcorn and spinach leaves and toss lightly. Shell the eggs, cut into wedges and arrange on top of the pasta. Slice the duck breasts, then place them on top of the salad. Beat the dressing ingredients together in a bowl until well blended, then drizzle over the salad. Serve immediately.

Shredded Duck in Lettuce Leaves

Serves 4–6

15 g/¹/₂ oz dried Chinese (shiitake)
mushrooms
2 tbsp vegetable oil
400 g/14 oz skinless, boneless duck
breast, cut crossways into thin strips
1 red chilli, deseeded and diagonally
sliced thinly
4–6 spring onions, trimmed and
diagonally sliced
2 garlic cloves, peeled and crushed
75 g/3 oz beansprouts
3 tbsp soy sauce
1 tbsp Chinese rice wine or dry sherry
1–2 tsp clear honey or brown sugar
4–6 tbsp hoisin sauce
large, crisp lettuce leaves. such as
iceberg or cos
handful fresh mint leaves
sweet chilli dipping sauce, to serve

Cover the dried Chinese mushrooms with almost-boiling water, leave
for 20 minutes, then drain and slice thinly.

Heat a large wok, add the oil and, when hot, stir-fry the duck for
3–4 minutes until sealed. Remove with a slotted spoon and reserve.

Add the chilli, spring onions, garlic and Chinese mushrooms to the
wok and stir-fry for 2–3 minutes until softened.

Add the beansprouts, the soy sauce, Chinese rice wine or dry sherry
and honey or brown sugar to the wok, and continue to stir-fry for
1 minute, or until blended.

Stir in the reserved duck and stir-fry for 2 minutes, or until well mixed
together and heated right through. Transfer to a warmed serving dish.

Arrange the hoisin sauce in a small bowl on a tray or plate with a pile
of lettuce leaves and the mint leaves.

Let each guest spoon a little hoisin sauce onto a lettuce leaf, then top
with a large spoonful of the stir-fried duck and vegetables and roll up
the leaf to enclose the filling. Serve with the sweet chilli dipping sauce.

Warm Chard Salad with Anchovies Garlic

Serves 4

1 medium onion, peeled and sliced
2–3 garlic cloves
3 tbsp olive oil
175 g/6 oz feta cheese
2 x 50 g/2 oz cans anchovy fillets
350 g/12 oz Swiss chard, preferably
young leaves
salt and freshly ground
black pepper

Peel the onion and slice thinly, then peel the garlic and slice.

Heat 2 tablespoons of the oil in a pan, add the onion and garlic and cook over a gentle heat, stirring frequently, for 10–12 minutes until the onion is tender. Keep warm.

Drain the cheese, cut into small cubes, and reserve. Drain the anchovy fillets and cut the fillets in half, if liked.

The variety of chard you use will dictate its preparation method. If using rainbow chard, this has an attractive red stalk down the centre of each leaf. Cut the red stalk out and cook separately from the leaves. They will take about 3–4 minutes. This applies to older chard leaves as well. Younger chard leaves will take less time.

Thoroughly rinse the chard and, if the leaves are large, then cut them in half or quarters depending on size. Bring a large pan of lightly salted water to the boil, add the chard and cook for 1–3 minutes until tender. Drain and return to the pan. Add the onion and garlic together with the anchovy fillets and seasoning to taste and stir lightly together. Spoon into a serving dish and top with the feta cheese. Drizzle with the remaining oil, season with black pepper and serve while still warm.

Warm Swordfish Niçoise

Serves 4

4 swordfish steaks, about 2.5 cm/
1 in thick, weighing about
175 g/6 oz each
juice of 1 lime
2 tbsp olive oil
salt and freshly ground black pepper
400 g/14 oz farfalle
225 g/8 oz French beans, topped
and cut in half
1 tsp Dijon mustard
2 tsp white wine vinegar
pinch caster sugar
3 tbsp olive oil
225 g/8 oz ripe tomatoes, quartered
50 g/2 oz pitted black olives
2 medium eggs, hard-boiled and
quartered
8 anchovy fillets, drained and cut in
half lengthways

Place the swordfish steaks in a shallow dish. Mix the lime juice with the oil, season to taste with salt and pepper and spoon over the steaks. Turn the steaks to coat them evenly. Cover and place in the refrigerator to marinate for 1 hour.

Bring a large pan of lightly salted water to a rolling boil. Add the farfalle and cook according to the packet instructions, or until *al dente*. Add the French beans about 4 minutes before the end of the cooking time.

Mix the mustard, vinegar and sugar together in a small jug. Gradually whisk in the olive oil to make a thick dressing.

Cook the swordfish in a griddle pan or under a hot preheated grill for 2 minutes on each side, or until just cooked through; overcooking will make it tough and dry. Remove and cut into 2 cm/³/₄ inch chunks.

Drain the pasta and beans thoroughly and place in a large bowl. Pour over the dressing and toss to coat. Add the cooked swordfish, tomatoes, olives, hard-boiled eggs and anchovy fillets. Gently toss together, taking care not to break up the eggs.

Tip into a warmed serving bowl or divide the pasta between individual plates. Serve immediately.

Spicy Prawns in Lettuce Cups

Serves 4

1 lemongrass stalk
225 g/8 oz peeled cooked prawns
1 tsp finely grated lime zest
1 red bird's-eye chilli, deseeded and
finely chopped
2.5 cm/1 in piece fresh root ginger,
peeled and grated
2 little gem lettuces, divided
into leaves
25 g/1 oz roasted peanuts, chopped
2 spring onions, trimmed and
diagonally sliced
fresh coriander sprig, to garnish

For the coconut sauce:

2 tbsp freshly grated or
unsweetened shredded coconut
1 tbsp hoisin sauce
1 tbsp light soy sauce
1 tbsp Thai fish sauce
1 tbsp palm sugar or soft light
brown sugar

Remove three or four of the tougher outer leaves of the lemongrass and reserve for another dish. Finely chop the remaining softer centre. Place 2 teaspoons of the chopped lemongrass in a bowl with the prawns, grated lime zest, chilli and ginger. Mix together to coat the prawns. Cover and place in the refrigerator to marinate while you make the coconut sauce.

For the sauce, place the grated coconut in a wok or nonstick frying pan and dry-fry for 2–3 minutes until golden. Remove from the pan and reserve. Add the hoisin, soy and fish sauces to the pan with the sugar and 4 tablespoons water. Simmer for 2–3 minutes, then remove from the heat. Leave to cool.

Pour the sauce over the prawns, add the toasted coconut and toss to mix together. Divide the prawn and coconut sauce mixture between the lettuce leaves and arrange on a platter.

Sprinkle over the chopped roasted peanuts and spring onions and garnish with a sprig of fresh coriander. Serve immediately.

Warm Lobster Salad with Hot Thai Dressing

Serves 4

1 orange; 50 g/2 oz granulated sugar; 2 cos lettuce hearts, shredded; 1 small avocado, peeled and thinly sliced; $^1/_2$ cucumber, peeled, deseeded and thinly sliced; 1 ripe mango, peeled, stoned and thinly sliced; 1 tbsp butter or vegetable oil 1 large lobster, meat removed and cut into bite-size pieces; 2 tbsp Thai or Italian basil leaves; 4 large cooked prawns, peeled, with tails left on, to garnish

For the dressing:

1 tbsp vegetable oil
4–6 spring onions, trimmed and sliced diagonally into 5 cm/2 in pieces
2.5 cm/1 in piece fresh root ginger, peeled and grated
1 garlic clove, peeled and crushed
grated zest of 1 lime
juice of 2–3 small limes
2 tbsp Thai fish sauce
1 tbsp brown sugar
1–2 tsp sweet chilli sauce, or to taste
1 tbsp sesame oil

With a sharp knife, cut the orange zest into thin julienne strips, then cook in boiling water for 2 minutes.

Drain the orange strips, then plunge under cold running water, drain and return to the saucepan with the sugar and 1 cm/$^1/_2$ inch water. Simmer until soft, then add 1 tablespoon cold water to stop the cooking. Remove from the heat and reserve. Arrange the lettuce on four large plates and arrange the avocado, cucumber and mango slices over the lettuce.

Heat a wok or large frying pan, add the butter or oil and, when hot but not sizzling, add the lobster and stir-fry for 1–2 minutes until heated through. Remove and drain on absorbent kitchen paper.

To make the dressing, heat the vegetable oil in a wok, then add the spring onions, ginger and garlic and stir-fry for 1 minute. Add the lime zest, lime juice, fish sauce, sugar and chilli sauce. Stir until the sugar has dissolved. Remove from the heat, then add the sesame oil with the orange zest and liquor.

Arrange the lobster meat over the salad and drizzle with the dressing. Sprinkle with basil leaves, garnish with prawns and serve immediately.

Spiced Couscous Vegetables

Serves 4

1 tbsp olive oil
1 large shallot, peeled and finely chopped
1 garlic clove, peeled and finely chopped
1 small red pepper, deseeded and cut into strips
1 small yellow pepper, deseeded and cut into strips
1 small aubergine, diced
1 tsp each turmeric, ground cumin, ground cinnamon and paprika
2 tsp ground coriander
large pinch saffron strands
2 tomatoes, peeled, deseeded and diced
2 tbsp lemon juice
225 g/8 oz couscous
225 ml/8 fl oz vegetable stock
2 tbsp raisins
2 tbsp whole almonds
2 tbsp freshly chopped parsley
2 tbsp freshly chopped coriander
salt and freshly ground black pepper

Heat the oil in a large frying pan, add the shallot and garlic and cook for 2–3 minutes until softened. Add the peppers and aubergine and reduce the heat. Cook for 8–10 minutes until the vegetables are tender, adding a little water if necessary.

Test a piece of aubergine to ensure it is cooked through. Add all the spices and cook for a further minute, stirring. Increase the heat and add the tomatoes and lemon juice. Cook for 2–3 minutes until the tomatoes have started to collapse. Remove from the heat and leave to cool slightly.

Meanwhile, put the couscous into a large bowl. Bring the stock to the boil in a saucepan, then pour over the couscous. Stir well and cover with a clean tea towel. Leave to stand for 7–8 minutes until all the stock is absorbed and the couscous is tender.

Uncover the couscous and fluff with a fork. Stir in the vegetable and spice mixture along with the raisins, almonds, parsley and coriander. Season to taste with salt and pepper and serve.

Warm Fruity Rice Salad

Serves 4

175 g/6 oz mixed basmati
and wild rice
125 g/4 oz skinless chicken breast
300 ml/½ pint chicken or
vegetable stock
125 g/4 oz ready-to-eat
dried apricots
125 g/4 oz ready-to-eat dried dates
3 celery stalks

For the dressing:

2 tbsp sunflower oil
1 tbsp white wine vinegar
4 tbsp lemon juice
1–2 tsp clear honey, warmed
1 tsp Dijon mustard
freshly ground black pepper

To garnish:

6 spring onions
fresh coriander sprigs

Place the rice in a pan of boiling salted water and cook for
15–20 minutes until tender. Rinse thoroughly with boiling water
and reserve.

Meanwhile, wipe the chicken and place in a shallow saucepan with
the stock. Bring to the boil, cover and simmer for about 15 minutes
until the chicken is cooked thoroughly and the juices run clear.

Leave the chicken in the stock until cool enough to handle, then cut
into thin slices.

Chop the apricots and dates into small pieces. Peel any tough
membranes from the outside of the celery and chop into dice. Fold
the apricots, dates, celery and sliced chicken into the warm rice.

Make the dressing by whisking all the ingredients together in a small
bowl until mixed thoroughly. Pour 2–3 tablespoons over the rice and
stir in gently and evenly. Serve the remaining dressing separately.

Trim and chop the spring onions. Sprinkle the spring onions over the
top of the salad and garnish with the sprigs of coriander. Serve while
still warm.

Warm Leek Tomato Salad

Serves 4

450 g/1 lb trimmed baby leeks
225 g/8 oz ripe but firm tomatoes
2 shallots, peeled and cut
into thin wedges

For the honey and lime dressing:

2 tbsp clear honey
grated zest of 1 lime
4 tbsp lime juice
1 tbsp light olive oil
1 tsp Dijon mustard
salt and freshly ground
black pepper

To garnish:

freshly chopped tarragon
freshly chopped basil

Trim the leeks so that they are all the same length. Place in a steamer over a pan of boiling water and steam for 8 minutes, or until just tender.

Drain the leeks thoroughly and arrange in a shallow serving dish.

Make a cross in the tops of the tomatoes, place in a bowl and cover them with boiling water until their skins start to peel away. Remove from the bowl and carefully remove the skins.

Cut the tomatoes into quarters and remove the seeds, then chop into small dice. Spoon over the top of the leeks together with the shallots.

In a small bowl, make the dressing by whisking the honey, lime zest, lime juice, olive oil, mustard and salt and pepper. Pour 3 tablespoons of the dressing over the leeks and tomatoes and garnish with the tarragon and basil. Serve while the leeks are still warm, with the remaining dressing served separately.

Baby Roast Potato Salad

Serves 4

350 g/12 oz small shallots
900 g/2 lb small even-sized
new potatoes
2 tbsp olive oil
sea salt and freshly ground
black pepper
2 medium courgettes
175 g/6 oz cherry tomatoes
2 fresh rosemary sprigs
150 ml/¹/₄ pint soured cream
2 tbsp freshly snipped chives

Preheat the oven to 200°C/400°F/Gas Mark 6. Trim the shallots, but leave the skins on. Put in a saucepan of lightly salted boiling water with the potatoes and cook for 5 minutes; drain. Separate the shallots and plunge them into cold water for 1 minute.

Put the oil on a baking sheet lined with foil or a roasting tin and heat for a few minutes. Peel the skins off the shallots – they should now come away easily. Add to the baking sheet or roasting tin with the potatoes and toss in the oil to coat. Sprinkle with a little sea salt. Roast the potatoes and shallots in the preheated oven for 10 minutes.

Meanwhile, trim the courgettes, halve lengthways and cut into 5 cm/ 2 inch chunks. Add to the baking sheet or roasting tin, toss to mix and cook for 5 minutes.

Pierce the tomato skins with a sharp knife. Add to the sheet or tin with the rosemary and cook for a further 5 minutes, or until all the vegetables are tender. Remove the rosemary and discard. Grind a little black pepper over the vegetables.

Spoon into a wide serving bowl. Mix together the sour cream and chives and drizzle over the vegetables just before serving.

Warm Potato, Pear Pecan Salad

Serves 4

900 g/2 lb new potatoes, preferably
red-skinned, unpeeled
1 tsp Dijon mustard
2 tsp white wine vinegar
3 tbsp groundnut oil
1 tbsp hazelnut or walnut oil
2 tsp poppy seeds
salt and freshly ground
black pepper
2 firm ripe dessert pears
2 tsp lemon juice
175 g/6 oz baby spinach leaves
75 g/3 oz toasted pecan nuts

Scrub the potatoes, then cook in a saucepan of lightly salted boiling water for 15 minutes, or until tender. Drain, cut into halves, or quarters if large, and place in a serving bowl.

In a small bowl or jug, whisk together the mustard and vinegar. Gradually add the oils until the mixture begins to thicken. Stir in the poppy seeds and season to taste with salt and pepper.

Pour about two thirds of the dressing over the hot potatoes and toss gently to coat. Leave until the potatoes have soaked up the dressing and are just warm.

Meanwhile, quarter and core the pears. Cut into thin slices, then sprinkle with the lemon juice to prevent them from going brown. Add to the potatoes with the spinach leaves and toasted pecan nuts. Gently mix together.

Drizzle the remaining dressing over the salad and serve immediately, before the spinach starts to wilt.

Mediterranean Potato Salad

Serves 4

700 g/1¹/₂ lb small, waxy potatoes
2 red onions, peeled and
roughly chopped
1 yellow pepper, deseeded and
roughly chopped
1 green pepper, deseeded and
roughly chopped
6 tbsp extra virgin olive oil
125 g/4 oz ripe tomatoes, chopped
50 g/2 oz pitted black olives, sliced
125 g/4 oz feta cheese
3 tbsp freshly chopped parsley
2 tbsp white wine vinegar
1 tsp Dijon mustard
1 tsp clear honey
salt and freshly ground
black pepper
fresh parsley sprigs, to garnish

Preheat the oven to 200°C/400°F/Gas Mark 6. Place the potatoes in a large saucepan of salted water, bring to the boil and simmer until just tender. Do not overcook. Drain and plunge into cold water to stop them from cooking further.

Place the onions in a bowl with the yellow and green peppers, then pour over 2 tablespoons of the olive oil. Stir and spoon onto a large baking tray. Cook in the preheated oven for 25–30 minutes until the vegetables are tender and lightly charred in places, stirring occasionally. Remove from the oven and transfer to a large bowl.

Cut the potatoes into bite-size pieces and mix with the roasted onions and peppers. Add the tomatoes and olives to the potatoes. Crumble over the feta cheese and sprinkle with the chopped parsley.

Whisk together the remaining olive oil, vinegar, mustard and honey, then season to taste with salt and pepper. Pour the dressing over the potatoes and toss gently together. Garnish with parsley sprigs and serve immediately.

Hot Grilled Chicory Pears

Serves 4

50 g/2 oz unblanched almonds,
roughly chopped
4 small heads chicory
2 tbsp olive oil
1 tbsp walnut oil
2 firm, ripe dessert pears
2 tsp lemon juice
1 tsp freshly chopped oregano.
salt and freshly ground
black pepper
freshly chopped oregano, to garnish
warm ciabatta bread, to serve

Preheat the grill. Spread the chopped almonds in a single layer on the grill pan. Cook under a hot grill for about 3 minutes, moving the almonds around occasionally, until lightly browned. Reserve.

Halve the chicory lengthways and cut out the cores. Mix together the olive and walnut oils. Brush about 2 tablespoons all over the chicory.

Put the chicory in the grill pan, cut-side up, and cook under a hot grill for 2–3 minutes until beginning to char. Turn and cook for a further 1–2 minutes, then turn again.

Peel, core and thickly slice the pears. Brush with 1 tablespoon of the oils, then place the pears on top of the chicory. Grill for a further 3–4 minutes until both the chicory and pears are soft.

Transfer the chicory and pears to four warmed serving plates. Whisk together the remaining oil, lemon juice and oregano and season to taste with salt and pepper.

Drizzle the dressing over the chicory and pears and scatter with the toasted almonds. Garnish with fresh oregano and serve with ciabatta bread.

Warm Noodle Salad with Sesame Peanut Dressing

Serves 4

125 g/4 oz smooth peanut butter
6 tbsp sesame oil
3 tbsp light soy sauce
2 tbsp red wine vinegar
1 tbsp freshly grated root ginger
2 tbsp double cream
250 g pack Chinese fine egg noodles
125 g/4 oz beansprouts
225 g/8 oz baby sweetcorn
125 g/4 oz carrots, peeled and cut into matchsticks
125 g/4 oz mangetout
125 g/4 oz cucumber, cut into thin strips
3 spring onions, trimmed and finely shredded

Place the peanut butter, 4 tablespoons of the sesame oil, the soy sauce, vinegar and ginger in a food processor. Blend until smooth, then stir in 75 ml/3 fl oz hot water and blend again. Pour in the cream, then blend briefly until smooth. Pour the dressing into a jug and reserve.

Bring a saucepan of lightly salted water to the boil, add the noodles and beansprouts and cook for 4 minutes, or according to the packet instructions. Drain, rinse under cold running water and drain again. Stir in the remaining sesame oil and keep warm.

Bring a saucepan of lightly salted water to the boil and add the baby sweetcorn, carrots and mangetout and cook for 3–4 minutes until just tender but still crisp. Drain and cut the mangetout in half. Slice the baby sweetcorn (if very large) into 2–3 pieces and arrange on a warmed serving dish with the noodles. Add the cucumber strips and spring onions. Spoon over a little of the dressing and serve immediately with the remaining dressing.

Cooked Vegetable Salad with Satay Sauce

Serves 4

125 ml/4 fl oz groundnut oil
225 g/8 oz unsalted peanuts
1 onion, peeled and finely chopped
1 garlic clove, peeled and crushed
$^1/_2$ tsp chilli powder
1 tsp ground coriander
$^1/_2$ tsp ground cumin
$^1/_2$ tsp sugar
1 tbsp dark soy sauce
2 tbsp fresh lemon juice
2 tbsp light olive oil
salt and freshly ground black pepper
125 g/4 oz French green beans, trimmed and halved
125 g/4 oz carrots
125 g/4 oz cauliflower florets
125 g/4 oz broccoli florets
125 g/4 oz Chinese leaves or pak choi, trimmed and shredded
125 g/4 oz beansprouts
1 tbsp sesame oil
fresh watercress sprigs and cucumber, cut into slivers, to garnish

Heat a wok, add the oil and, when hot, add the peanuts and stir-fry for 3–4 minutes. Drain on absorbent kitchen paper and leave to cool. Blend to a fine powder in a food processor.

Place the onion and garlic with the spices, sugar, soy sauce, lemon juice and olive oil in a food processor. Season to taste with salt and pepper, then process into a paste. Transfer to the wok and stir-fry for 3–4 minutes.

Stir 600 ml/1 pint hot water into the paste and bring to the boil. Add the ground peanuts and simmer gently for 5–6 minutes until the mixture thickens. Reserve the satay sauce.

Cook the vegetables in batches in lightly salted boiling water. Cook the French beans, carrots, cauliflower and broccoli for 3–4 minutes, and the Chinese leaves or pak choi and beansprouts for 2 minutes. Drain each batch, drizzle over the sesame oil and arrange on a large, warmed serving dish. Garnish with watercress sprigs and cucumber. Serve with the satay sauce.

Index

Index